PARENT'S GUIDE

Active Parenting

of

Teens

Third Edition

Michael H. Popkin, PhD

ACTIVE PARENTING™
PUBLISHERS

❖

to the memory of

Bernard Howard

(1916 to 1989)

There are those who throw bricks through the dreams of others and those who provide bricks for others to build their dreams. Bernie Howard was a dream builder. Whenever someone came to him with an earnest dream that could help others, his position was always, *How can I help?* Whether it was providing dignified care for the elderly, shelter for the homeless, or a new approach to parent education, Bernie Howard reached for his checkbook when others reached for the door. When his advice was needed for writing a business plan or planning a building project, he was never too busy. He was there.

His contribution to the founding of Active Parenting Publishers is remembered in this dedication. May his memory live as long as caring people continue to support those who care about children and teens.

❖

ISBN 10: 1-59723-231-9 / ISBN-13: 978-1-59723-231-9

Table of Contents

Contents

Also by Michael H. Popkin

PARENTING PROGRAMS

(Complete curriculums that include a Parent Guide,
Leader's Guide, and Video)

Active Parenting Now: For Parents of Children Ages 5 to 12

Active Parenting for Stepfamilies
(with Elizabeth Einstein)

1,2,3,4 Parents! Parenting Children Ages 1 to 4
(with Marilyn Montgomery and Betsy Gard)

Parents on Board: Building Academic Success Through Parent Involvement
(with Bettie B. Youngs and Jane M. Healy)

Free The Horses: A Self-Esteem Adventure
(with Susan D. Greathead)

Active Teaching

Windows: Healing and Helping Through Loss
(with Mary Joe Hannaford)

BOOKS

Taming the Spirited Child

DocPop's 52 Weeks of Active Parenting

Getting Through to Your Kids (with Robyn Spizman)

Active Parenting: Teaching Courage, Cooperation and Responsibility

Quality Parenting (with Linda Albert)

So...Why Aren't You Perfect Yet?

**For more information about these and other resources or to find a
parenting class near you, go to www.ActiveParenting.com**

Acknowledgements

This revision of *Active Parenting of Teens*, like its predecessor, is based largely on the theories of Alfred Adler and Rudolf Dreikurs, two of the truly great psychological thinkers of the 20th Century. Their principles and methods have proven effective with millions of parents and educators, and the field of parent education is greatly in their debt. Where I have extended these theories and methods, I tread lightly with the utmost respect for their genius and contribution.

To complement the Adlerian base of this program I have included work derived from communication theorists such as Tom Gordon, Carl Rogers, and Robert Carkuff. The combination of such empathy training with Adlerian parenting methods represents a very powerful parenting model that can be taught to all parents living in a democratic society. The *Active Parenting of Teens* program, along with its companion program *Active Parenting Now* (for parents of children five to twelve), have been used successfully by more than three million parents in countries all over the world since 1983.

While writing this revision I was fortunate to have an extraordinarily talented advisory board comprised of parent and family service professionals, Active Parenting class leaders, and parents of teens to help me update and improve the original program. Their input and feedback made this a much better program.

We also gathered the input of families nationwide, who wrote to us about their daily conflicts. Their lives became the basis of the stories you'll read in this book. Additional input came from Active Parenting class leaders, whose daily interaction with parents gives them insight into the issues that are important to today's families. Their support of parent education is lived every day in hundreds of behind-the-scenes ways.

A huge acknowledgement and appreciation goes to the Product Development Department at Active Parenting: Manager Molly Davis shepherded the project from start to finish; Art Director Gabrielle Tingley created a vibrant new look for the program; and Coordinator Rhea Lewis-Ngcobo supported us all with patience and adaptability. Marketing Manager Virginia Murray contributed much to the project, as well, with her superior ability to see the big picture while attending to countless details. Our team's attention to detail, commitment to excellence, long hours and hard work have made this a program of which we can truly be proud.

Finally, to my parents, Harry and Naomi Popkin, my wife, Melody, and children, Megan and Ben (Matt Shelton in the video): thank you for your support of Active Parenting, your involvement in this project, and most of all, for your love.

Michael Popkin, Atlanta, 2008

Introduction

"We are all here because we are scared to death about what our children will do when they become teenagers." These words, spoken by a father in a parenting group that I led some years ago, are as timely today as they were then. We were dealing with parenting issues that related to five-year-olds, and yet the parents' motivation for learning was fear of the teen years.

And why not? The statistics on teen drug use, pregnancy, delinquency, and even suicide are enough to give any concerned parent pause for reflection. *Am I doing all that I can to prepare my teen to face these dangers?* Although we can never guarantee our children's success, we want to know in our hearts that we have given them our best efforts.

Part of giving our best means tackling the job of parenting like we would any other job that is both important and difficult—with training and support. For too long, however, our society has treated parenting as if it were either easy or unimportant, and parents have had to fend for themselves. Without training, families often experience frustration and conflict, and they're left wondering what went wrong.

Fortunately, there are answers. Parents and parent-education professionals have learned a lot over the years about what works and what doesn't work with teenagers. They have partnered with institutions that serve families to offer parent-education programs such as *Active Parenting of Teens*. They've committed themselves to making a difference.

When I founded Active Parenting Publishers in 1980, I was working as a child and family therapist. Part of my job was to provide counseling and therapy to individuals and families, and the other part was to provide parent-education courses and school consultation in the community. Over the years, I experienced firsthand the power effective parenting methods have to change the lives of parents and children. I saw unmotivated and unruly teenagers respond positively when their parents began to use these methods. I saw parents who had grown angry and distant "reawaken the feeling of love for my children," as one mother so poetically said.

Motivated by the knowledge that I had the right approach to parenting, I set out to develop a delivery system that would make these skills come alive for parents—one that would demonstrate these methods and make them easier to learn. The result was the original *Active Parenting Discussion Program*, the world's first video-based parent-education program. The response was beyond my imagination as Active Parenting courses began to spring up throughout North America.

Since then, the original program has been replaced by three different programs: *1, 2, 3, 4 Parents!* (for parents of 1- to 4-year-olds), *Active Parenting Now* (for parents of 5- to 12-year-olds), and *Active Parenting of Teens* (for parents of teens and tweens). To date more than three million parents have completed at least one of these courses, with millions of others having experienced the Video Library versions of the programs on television. These courses have now been translated into multiple foreign languages and are used in countries all over the world.

We developed the first edition of *Active Parenting of Teens* in 1988 and revised it in 1998. The book you hold in your hands represents the third edition of this popular program. It contains all the information and practical skills from the program. Some of these methods will take time to implement, but this investment of yourself now will save you and your family much time, frustration, and heartache later.

This book is your parenting resource. However, some of what you will read may not fit your own view of parenting. I hope you will keep an open mind and consider these ideas fairly. In the final analysis, you are the authority in your family. Feel free to pick and choose from this program what feels right to you, or, as one parent so aptly put it, "Use the best and let go of the rest."

I wish you and your family much joy as you travel these exciting years together.

Michael H. Popkin, Ph.D.

You Are Welcome Here

White collar, blue collar, no collar
If you are a parent
You are welcome here.
Calm and cool or hot-under-the-collar
If you care for children
You are welcome here.
Traditional family: husband and wife,
Single, remarried, or partnered for life
If you love your child
You are welcome here.
Whatever your race
From wherever you hale
Whatever your faith (or lack thereof)
Regardless of creed, or past misdeeds,
If you're willing to learn
You are welcome here.
Mom, dad, uncle or granny
Pull up a chair
Let down your hair
And if you don't have any
You're still welcome here!

Michael H. Popkin
Founder,
Active Parenting Publishers

The Active Parent

The conventional wisdom about parenting teenagers seems to be that it is a necessary evil, something to be dreaded, feared, and undertaken with all the enthusiasm of a root canal without Novocaine. The jokes about parenting teenagers are all negative: "It's like trying to nail Jell-o to a tree;" "It explains why some animals eat their young;" "There's nothing wrong with teenagers that reasoning with them won't aggravate." Parents have been told for so long that teenage rebellion is a necessary part of growing up that they expect a period of turmoil and confusion followed by an overnight transformation into adulthood and maturity. They hold their breath and wait for the tide of hormones to rise, do its worst, and finally recede.

Parenting isn't the only influence on your teen's development, but it's the one you can do the most about.

The problem with this negative expectation theory of adolescence is that it does not explain why many teenagers make a smooth transition from childhood to adulthood, enriching their families and communities along the way, and handling the challenges of growing up with courage, even grace. My wife and I have raised two teens of our own, and we would not have traded the experience for anything. What enables some families to make the journey through adolescence so well? Part of it is luck: good genes and good circumstances. Another part has to do with the fact that some teens are able to figure it out on their own and make good decisions in spite of events beyond their control. The rest has to do with good parenting. This is the realm of *Active Parenting of Teens*. It is based on the belief that parenting isn't the only influence on your teen's development, but it's the one you can do the most about.

Another Tough Century for Teenagers

The world of the 21st century is tough on teenagers. First and foremost, it's a dangerous place to grow up. Violence against teens—often by other teens—is so rampant that in many schools, teens are afraid to go to the rest room for fear of being harassed, extorted, injured, or worse. Stories of mass school shootings haunt the minds of many students who remember the images of places like Columbine and Virginia Tech all too well. Teen role models too often promote lives of crime and violence in a world where guns are accessible to minors and gang involvement has spread beyond the inner city.

Substance abuse continues to plague teenagers in our neighborhoods and throughout the world, as more and more teens succumb to the temptation and pressure to use tobacco, alcohol, and other drugs. These seemingly cheap thrills often have regrettable and lasting effects: damaged relationships, bad grades, risky sexual encounters, criminal records. Many become overdose victims, addicts, car crash statistics, school drop-outs, and other casualties of high-risk lifestyles.

Our society, with its in-your-face media style, bombards teens with messages about sexuality, appearance, and the importance of being "hot." No wonder more than a million teenage girls get pregnant each year and thousands suffer from eating disorders such as bulimia (bingeing and purging) and anorexia (self-starvation). Boys are not immune to these messages either, with many using steroids and going to extremes to get that "buff" look that will help them attract sexual partners. Thousands of teens contract STDs (sexually transmitted diseases) each year. Many more have sex but have no idea how to have a respectful, loving relationship or to take responsibility for their unplanned offspring.

Teens today are maturing faster than ever, with the average age of puberty dropping with each new generation. Many eleven-year-old girls are now young women biologically yet still children emotionally. By age fifteen or sixteen, teens often lose patience with adult-imposed rules and expectations. Yet they are going through so much change—physical, emotional, social, and intellectual—that they still need adult guidance and support. Feeling too old for rules and too young for true independence, many teens are confused and frustrated.

Teens today are more likely than ever before to have parents who are divorced. Many live in single-parent homes, where financial pressure and inadequate supervision are common problems. Others have to deal with their parents' remarriages and their conflicting emotions at the introduction of new stepparents and perhaps new siblings to their lives.

More teens live in two-career families than ever before. Although this trend is positive in many ways, parental support and supervision—vital for these growing young people—is often lacking when both parents work. In one study, parents in dual-career families spent an average of just five minutes a week with their teens!

The demands of an increasingly technological society mean that education is more important than ever, yet teens are dropping out of high school in record numbers, and many of those who stay graduate without really learning the fundamentals of reading and math. Others go on to college but gain no sense of the value and requirements of work. When they enter the working world, they often flounder from job to job, unsatisfied and unproductive.

Half a million teenagers attempt suicide each year. The fact that a relatively small percentage of these teens actually die in this tragic way suggests that most kids are not really ready to give up… but they are crying for help.

Some Facts about Drug Use, Sexuality, and Violence among U.S. Teens

- In the United States, there are 10 million+ drinkers between ages 12 and 20. [1]

- 23% of high school students currently smoke cigarettes. 80% of smokers began smoking before age 18. [2]

- 50% of teens have tried an illicit drug by the end of high school. [3]

- 47% of high school students have had sexual intercourse. Of that group, 37% did not use a condom at least once. [2]

- 24% of girls ages 15-17 reported that drinking or drug use had led them to "do more" sexually than they had planned or have unprotected sex. [4]

- 31% of women become pregnant at least once before age 20. 80% of these pregnancies are unintended, and 81 percent of these young women are unmarried. [5]

- Teens have the highest rate of STDs of any age group: 1 in every 4 teens gets an STD by age 21. [4]

- 23% of youths ages 12-17 reported that they had gotten into a serious fight at school or work in the past year. [1]

- 26% of 14- to 17-year-old boys said they or their friends had been the victims of gang violence. [2]

[1] Substance Abuse and Mental Health Services Administration (SAMHSA), *2005 National Survey on Drug Use and Health*, 2006

[2] Centers for Disease Control (CDC) *Youth Risk Behavior Surveillance Report*, 2005

[3] National Institute on Drug Abuse *Monitoring the Future* report, 2005

[4] Kaiser Family Foundation. *Substance Use and Risky Sexual Behavior: Attitudes and Practices Among Adolescents and Young Adults.* Menlo Park, CA: The Jenry J. Kaiser Foundation, 2002

[5] National Campaign to Prevent Teen Pregnancy Analysis of Teen Pregnancy Data, 2006

The Good News

So it's truer than ever that the teenage years are full of change and challenge. Nevertheless, we have learned a lot about what teens need from parents and others in order to have the best chance of success. This book will present a model for understanding and guiding teens that has been used effectively by more than three million parents in the U.S. and around the world. For reasons that will become clear as you continue to read, we call this model *Active Parenting*. The fact is that many families today not only help their children survive the dangerous teen years, but also give them the resources that enable them to go on and thrive. With the support of knowledgeable and caring parents and other adults, many teens do well at school and at home, plus find time for sports, volunteer work, and other worthwhile interests. Yes, these teens and their families still have problems—no family gets through the teen years without some lost sleep. But they also have the skills and support to manage their problems effectively before they escalate out of control.

Teens in these families receive many of the same negative messages from society that their more troubled peers do, but their parents have learned how to help them separate the positive values from the negative. These parents have learned how to listen to their teens in ways that promote respectful two-way communication. They have learned how to support their teens in solving problems. And they have learned effective methods of discipline that help their teens grow into responsible young adults.

If you approach the ideas presented here with an open mind, you will find ways of making these years some of the best that your family has ever experienced.

Active Parenting of Teens is based on a combination of theory, research, and practical experience and is designed to help you maximize your ability to influence your teens in a positive direction. It will help you deal with the daily hassles of family living and improve the overall relationships that you share with your teen and other family members. It will help you prepare your teens to become independent adults who have the skills and values to live fulfilling lives and make real contributions to their communities. And, if you approach the ideas presented here with an open mind, you will find ways of making these years some of the best that your family has ever experienced.

The Tasks of Adolescence

The first step in helping teens through these turbulent years is to learn something about what makes them tick. Psychological research over the last half century reveals that all teens have certain developmental "tasks" they are trying to accomplish—often subconsciously—as they mature towards adulthood. Tasks include:

- developing an identity independent of their parents in order to break away from them and then to re-establish themselves as their parents' peers.

- coming to terms with their emerging sexuality.

- coming to terms with the need to work.

- developing a philosophy of life and a value system upon which to make decisions.

One minute they may be loving children... and the next, raging aliens. Regardless, one thing remains constant: They need you to help guide and support them through this difficult time.

Completing these developmental tasks in our stressful modern society is a major challenge for all teenagers. Add to this challenge the complications caused by major hormonal changes and rapid physical growth, and it's no wonder that teens often act like they are on an emotional roller coaster. One minute they may be loving children snuggling next to you on the sofa, and the next, raging aliens upset because you won't let them go to a concert. Regardless, one thing remains constant: They need you to help guide and support them through this difficult time.

During the past decade, science has uncovered a lot about why teen-aged humans are often so temperamental and changeable. For starters, a rapid and intense period of brain growth occurs from age 11 to 14 (slightly earlier in girls than boys). This rapid growth—the largest since infancy!—is followed by a period of pruning that can last all the way to the mid- or late twenties.

During the pruning process, brain connections that are used become coated with a substance called *myelin* and grow stronger, while those that are not used are pruned back and lost.

This pruning occurs from the back of the brain to the front:

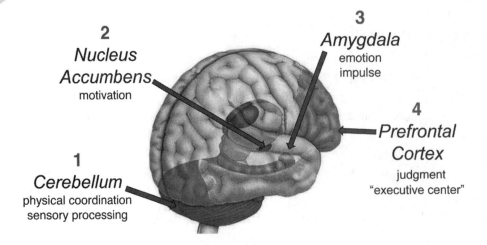

It starts with the *cerebellum*, which controls physical coordination and sensory processing... Then on to the *nucleus accumbens*, which handles motivation... Next to the *amygdala*, the seat of emotion... And last, but certainly not least, to the *prefrontal cortex*, the executive center of the brain that handles:

- Sound decision making

- Empathy

- Considering consequences

- Regulating emotions

- Self-awareness, and

- Morality

Sound like anybody you know? Think back to your own teen years and early twenties... Can you remember some of the foolish things you did ? We now know that at least part of "typical teenage behavior" is due to the fact that the brain's executive center is still developing. Most of the brain functions that you would associate with maturity and adulthood don't appear until the end of the pruning process, around age 25. This doesn't relieve teens of responsibility for their actions, but it does explain why parental supervision and guidance are still necessary throughout the teen years. The methods you will learn in this book will help you promote healthy growth and development of your teen's brain, strengthening positive neural connections and pruning away the weeds.

Teen Development

Do your teens do things that seem designed to drive you crazy? A lot of problematic teen behavior is rooted in struggles that all teens go through as part of the normal developmental process. Often this behavior is not a personal attack against parents (although it can seem like it is!).

Which of these characteristics are at the root of the particular problems your teen is experiencing?

Developmental Characteristics	Possible Behavior That Results
Pre-Teens	
Reproductive maturity reached: for girls, ages 8 ½ to 13; for boys, ages 9 ½ to 15	The beginning of sexual experimentation
Growing sense of independence and self-sufficiency	Starting to stray from family
Develop same-sex friendships and learn new social skills	May become very close to a best friend to the exclusion of the family
Develop more concrete logic skills	May use jokes that seem cruel to vent aggression
Young Teens (approx. 12 to 14 years)	
Rapid cycling through moods	Unpredictable and challenging behavior
Identity exploration begins	Experimentation with personality, peers, and appearance
Beginning concern with others' thoughts about them	General defensiveness due to strong feelings of self-consciousness
Developing capacity for critical analysis	Constant analysis and critique of family members
May believe they're invincible	Will reject adults' warnings about health and safety
Older Teens (approx. 15 to 18 years)	
Complete physical development	Struggle to integrate natural sexual and emotional needs with society's messages and their own values Struggle to react appropriately to being treated as an adult
Develop the ability to think abstractly	May use irony and other sophisticated forms of humor to critique society
Able to imagine the world as it should be and compare it to the way it is now	May become interested in making a difference in the world
Able to identify with other people's conditions	Become concerned about the feelings of others

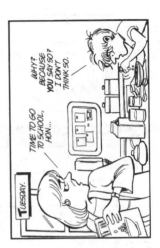

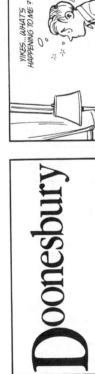

The Purpose of Parenting

The approach to parenting presented in this book is called "active" in contrast to what parents often do, which might be called "reactive." Reactive parenting is characterized by waiting until teens push parents to their limits, and then reacting with random discipline. This parenting style is usually fraught with frustration, anger, and escalating conflict. Reactive parenting unwittingly allows teens to control situations as well as parents' emotions. Instead of preventing or solving problems, this approach allows problems to continue, or even get worse, as parents and teens replay the same painful scenes over and over.

The philosophy of Active *Parenting of Teens* is that it is the job of the parent to play the leadership role in the family; however, this is not a simple matter of laying down the law. Effective leadership in any organization, from a business to a family, is a matter of having the right attitudes and skills.

Effective leadership in any organization, from a business to a family, is a matter of having the right attitudes and skills.

It involves:

- proactively anticipating and preventing problems.

- developing mutually respectful relationships.

- enforcing fair discipline.

- maintaining effective communication.

- using productive problem-solving methods.

- encouraging the participation and success of everyone involved.

This book will cover these skills and other parenting methods that I have adapted from the work of great psychologists such as Alfred Adler and Rudolf Dreikurs and organized into the Active Parenting method. Incidentally, parents have told me that the skills they learned in Active Parenting have not only made them more effective parents but have also made them better siblings, employees, managers, and friends.

Learn to catch your mistakes with a smile, not a kick. Encourage yourself for trying, and see what you can do differently next time. After all, mistakes are for learning.

Using the Active Parenting model will help improve relationships in your family, but don't expect change overnight. It will take a little practice and time, and you'll make mistakes. Remember, we all make mistakes when learning new skills. Don't be too hard on yourself, your partner, or your teens. Learn to catch your mistakes with a smile, not a kick. Encourage yourself for trying, and see what you can do differently next time. After all, mistakes are for learning. You may also recognize mistakes you have made in the past and mistakes your own parents made with you. It's helpful to recognize these mistakes because, again, you can learn from them. But it is important to let go of negative feelings such as guilt and resentment and use that energy to improve your own parenting now. If you have trouble letting go of such feelings on your own, sometimes individual or family counseling can be a great help.

Though society has become more stressful for teens and parents, the basic purpose of parenting has not changed. We can state it like this:

> *The purpose of parenting is to protect and prepare our children and teens to survive and thrive in the kind of society in which they will live.*

The dangers present in our modern society make it difficult to achieve the two goals in this definition: to protect and to prepare. We want to protect our teens so that they will survive. Yet if we protect them too much (overprotect them), we fail to prepare them to thrive on their own. Keep in mind that one of the objectives of parenting is to gradually work yourself out of a job!

What We Can Learn from a 17th-Century Swedish Battleship

In 1628, Sweden built one of the world's greatest battleships to date, the *Vasa*. The feature that made this ship so formidable was an upper deck of cannon in addition to the usual first deck. As the day of its launch grew near, the people of Stockholm, from nobles to townspeople, became more and more excited to see the mighty ship set sail. Finally, the day of its christening arrived and the *Vasa* took to the seas, hit a storm scarcely a mile out of the harbor, rolled over, and sank. The problem wasn't so much the storm—after all, other ships had withstood far worse storms. The problem was that the *Vasa* didn't have enough weight in its hull, or *ballast*, to counter the heavy upper row of cannon and stabilize itself. Lacking the proper ballast, the *Vasa* was no match for the storm's winds and waves. It simply toppled over and went down like a rock.

Think of your teen as a ship about to embark on the journey of a lifetime. He will be traveling through dangerous waters. What will help him make the right decision when he is offered drugs? How can you protect him when he is put into a physically dangerous situation, tempted to act out sexually, or come face to face with a host of other storms on the sea of adolescence? What will help him is the same thing that would have helped the *Vasa*: ballast—stabilizing weight at the teen's center. *Ballast*, in fact, is also defined as "that which gives stability to character." It's the core values that parents can help instill in teens—the stable character they will need to make good decisions when the waves get high and the winds blow hard.

What values and qualities of character are important for teens to develop?

To find the answer to this important question, we need to take another look at our purpose of parenting. If we are to protect and prepare our teens to survive and thrive in the kind of society in which they will live, we have to ask ourselves what it takes to survive and thrive in a fast paced, high tech, multi-cultural democracy. Do we want our teens to be people who will unquestioningly do as they're told, who are blindly obedient and fearful of authority? That might be useful if we were raising our teens to live under a dictatorship, but such qualities would not lead to success in a modern democratic society. Do we want teens who make their own rules and do as they wish? This might be useful if they lived in a lawless society, but in our society of laws, such teens could end up in prison—or dead.

There are many qualities of character that are important for surviving and thriving in a democratic society, but five seem to form the foundation upon which other qualities build. These five qualities of character will be the ballast in teens' ships that will keep them steady as they set out on their voyage.

Those who have the confidence to take worthwhile risks have the best chance to thrive. And when life gets tough, those with the courage to persevere are more likely to succeed.

Courage

A free society provides many opportunities for people to succeed, but success is not guaranteed, nor is it easy to attain. Those who have the confidence to take worthwhile risks have the best chance to thrive. And when life gets tough, those with the courage to persevere are more likely to succeed.

Among teenagers, it takes great courage to resist peer pressure, to stand up for oneself or for others, and to think independently. From the French word *coeur*, meaning heart, courage is a teen's inner strength. We will focus on ways of instilling this fundamental quality in Chapters 3 and 4.

Responsibility

Responsibility—a crucial concept in parenting—is the ability to recognize one's obligations, to know right from wrong, and to accept the consequences of one's decisions.

Once teens learn to take responsibility for their choices by experiencing the consequences that follow, they are equipped to make better choices. Many of the choices your teen has to make now may affect her entire life. She will be offered tobacco, alcohol, and other drugs, and she will choose to accept or decline. She will face choices about sex, about dropping out of school, about work and career, and perhaps even about whether to commit a crime. You won't be there, telling her what to do, but if you have prepared her to make responsible decisions and have instilled in her the courage to stand behind those decisions, she'll be prepared to meet her challenges. We will explore methods of teaching responsibility throughout this book, and especially in Chapter 3.

Cooperation

A teen who learns to live and work cooperatively with others has a much better chance to succeed than the lone wolf. Democracy is based on the notion that "none of us is as smart as all of us." Competition has its role in our society, but the individual who values teamwork is one who moves society forward.

Learning to cooperate begins in the family. Cooperation is fostered through everyday problem-solving and planning, which require effective communication and a spirit of mutual respect and participation. In Chapter 2 we will discover communication skills that will help you win the cooperation of your teen while teaching him to solve problems and make decisions cooperatively with others. And in every chapter, we will present a family meeting to encourage cooperation among all family members and a family enrichment activity to help you strengthen your relationship with your teen.

Respect

To treat others respectfully, and to expect them to treat you the same, makes way for the free sharing of ideas that eventually solve problems and create a better society for everyone.

The concept of mutual respect is a cornerstone of life in any democratic society, particularly one that includes a lot of diversity. To treat others respectfully, and to expect them to treat you the same, makes way for the free sharing of ideas that eventually solve problems and create a better society for everyone. On the other hand, lack of respect in a democratic society creates an atmosphere of resentment and hostility that leads to conflict and even aggression. Teaching our teens to respect us is only the beginning. Teaching them to respect all others, including themselves, is what will really make a difference.

Self-Esteem

Teens who believe they are worthwhile human beings, with talents and dreams that are worthy of respect, have the best chance of thriving. In fact, high self-esteem helps a person develop the other character traits that are needed to succeed: courage, responsibility, and cooperation. At the same time, seeing oneself as someone who embodies these positive qualities builds higher self-esteem. We will explore this cycle further in Chapter 4, as we look at how to help teens build self-esteem based on positive attitudes and actions, not self-hype.

High self-esteem helps a person develop the other character traits that are needed to succeed: courage, responsibility, and cooperation.

Of course, you will want to encourage your teen to develop additional values and qualities of character besides these essential five. The skills you learn here will prove effective for encouraging whatever values are important in your family. Of more immediate concern, these skills will also work to reduce the conflicts and hassles of everyday living with teenagers.

What skills will your teen need to succeed in the 21st-century workplace?

In addition to the ballast provided by a strong character, your teen will need sails to propel her forward as she completes her education and heads towards the world of work. In other words, your teen needs skills. Simply learning to repeat lists of facts is not going to cut it in the modern workplace. While knowledge is still important, of even greater value are skills such as:

- leadership
- negotiation
- goal setting and motivation
- creative thinking and problem solving
- communication (listening, speaking, and writing)
- the ability to learn

Encouraging your teen's development of these skills will give him a leg up when it comes to earning a living and finding meaningful work. Plus, it will boost your teen's self-esteem, giving him more personal power to resist the temptations of drugs, irresponsible sexuality, and violence.

Styles of Parenting

How you choose to guide your teen in the development of character, skills, and overall behavior is a matter of personal preference. No two parents are exactly alike, so no two parents will parent exactly alike. However, if we eliminate parents at the extremes—those who are overtly abusive or neglectful—the rest tend towards one of three major styles of parenting: an autocratic style (the "dictator"); a permissive style ("the doormat"); or an authoritative style ("the Active Parent"). Notice that I said "tend towards". The fact is that most people exhibit characteristics of all three parenting styles at different times, depending on their teen's behavior, their mood, and other factors. This inconsistency encourages their teens to test them to see how far they can push the limits. By understanding the three styles and knowing which one you tend towards, you'll have a better chance of applying the Active parenting style on a more consistent basis.

Most people exhibit characteristics of all three parenting styles at different times, depending on their teen's behavior, their mood, and other factors. This inconsistency encourages their teens to test them to see how far they can push the limits.

Before we go further, let's be clear: the Active Parenting method upholds the idea that parents are the leaders in the family, and teens are still in the role of learners. But keep this important principle of leadership in mind:

> *Leaders in a democratic society get their authority from those they lead.*

The same is true for parents. We are the authorities in our families, but to be effective, we must have the cooperation of our children and teens. Which leadership styles will foster this cooperation?

1. The Autocratic Style: The Dictator

The *autocratic* parent tries to be all-powerful in directing the lives of his children. This parent is usually a dominating, authoritarian figure who uses reward and punishment as tools to enforce his orders. Teens are kept in line by the threat of punishment if they misbehave and the promise of reward if they do what parents wish them to do. Teens are told what to do, how to do it, and where to do it. There is little or no room for them to question, challenge, or disagree. Sometimes, autocratic parents take a more subtle approach, using a combination of guilt, disapproval, and other emotional tactics to keep their kids in line. The common factor in all autocratic parents is a desire to control their teens.

Children brought up in autocratic families seldom thrive. Sometimes their spirits are broken and they give up. More often, they rebel. This rebellion can be characterized by sneaking or by open defiance. Rebellion usually happens during the teen years because by then the child has developed enough power—both physical and intellectual—to fight back. Autocratic parenting has been the typical parenting style for so many generations that teenage rebellion has come to be accepted by many experts as "normal." This is a mistake. Teenagers, as we will see, do not have to rebel to become independent.

The autocratic style of parenting can be described as "limits without freedom," which we can depict as a closed circle. This parenting method worked reasonably well when inequality was the norm in our society and the family patriarch dictated that children should be seen but not heard; however, it works poorly in today's world of increased equality. The autocratic parent deserves some credit for recognizing the need for limits and having the emotional strength to stand firm. But this parent goes much too far.

Autocratic Style
Limits without Freedom

You are tending toward the autocratic style of parenting when you say things like:

- "Because I'm the parent and I said so!"

- "As long as you live under my roof, you'll obey my rules."

- "When you are the parent, you can decide what to do."

and when you do things like:

- tell your teen what to wear.

- often find yourself angry and yelling.

- frequently ground or punish your teen in other ways.

2.   The Permissive Style: The Doormat

Permissive parents are often those who react strongly against the harsh and uncompromising autocratic method. Instead, they allow their teens to "do their own thing." In such households there is little respect for order and routine, and few limits are placed on anyone's freedom. Teens often have no curfew and few household responsibilities. They are pampered and, as a result, become accustomed to getting their own way. Permissive parents tend to behave like doormats, allowing their teens to walk all over them. Teens who grow up with this style of parenting may act like they enjoy the excessive freedom they are allowed, but without a clear authority figure to protect and guide them, underneath they feel insecure. Privately, they may even wish to have limits imposed on them. As one fifteen-year-old wrote in her blog, "I need rules. I need to hear someone say "no". I need a mom, not another friend." Teens with permissive parents sometimes lack a sense of belonging with the family, and because they have not learned to cooperate, they are often difficult to live with. They often rebel against authority or refuse to comply with rules. These unfortunate effects will follow them into adulthood where, accustomed to a lifestyle with no limits, they may have trouble keeping a job and struggle with the healthy "give and take" of close relationships.

The permissive method can be described as "freedom without limits" and shown as a zig-zag line, meaning freedom run rampant. Although it is commendable that permissive parents understand the need for freedom and are willing to share power with their children, they go too far also.

Permissive Style
Freedom without Limits

You are tending toward the permissive parenting style when you say things like:

- "I don't think that's a good idea... but, well... okay, if you really want to."

- "Do you really need this? Oh, all right. Here's the money."

- "I sure wish you'd pick up after yourself."

and when you do things like:

- ignore your teen's schoolwork until you see his low grades

- act as your teen's alarm clock and wake-up service.

- give in to her unreasonable demands because you're afraid she will become angry or sad.

3. The Authoritative Style: The Active Parent

The Active Parenting style is in some respects the middle ground between the autocratic method and permissive method. It is also much more. In an Active household, freedom is important, but so are the rights of others and the responsibilities of all. The parent is a leader who encourages order and routine and understands the need for reasonable limits to behavior. The Active Parenting method acknowledges a system of modern social equality in which every member of the family is important and worthy of respect.

Active Parenting acknowledges our democratic heritage and the role of social equality among all human beings in two important ways:

- Parents treat teens with dignity and respect, even during discipline.

- Teens are entitled to respectfully express their thoughts and feelings to their parents. In this way they are given the right to influence the decisions that affect their lives.

This is consistent with life in a democratic society:

Democracy does not meant that you will always get your way;
It means you will always get your say.

The Active method could be called "freedom within limits" and shown as a zig-zag line within the limits of a circle.

Active Style
Freedom <u>within</u> Limits

It would be appropriate to call the Active style "freedom within *expanding* limits," because as the teen grows up and assumes more responsibility, the authoritative parent gradually relaxes limits until the teenager (at age eighteen to twenty-one) has the same amount of independence as an adult. This is what is meant by expanding limits.

Freedom within Expanding Limits

You are tending toward the Active style of parenting when you say things like:

- "I know you're disappointed, but you can't go. Here's why..."

- "Sure we can talk about it. What's your idea?"

- "I know you can handle it. But if you need some help, just let me know."

and do things like:

- involve your teen in deciding who will do which family chores.

- give her responsibility over her homework, monitoring her just a little.

- show an active interest in his education by regularly discussing his subjects with him and attending school functions.

- talk with her about your expectations for her behavior and the consequences for breaking agreements.

- talk with him about topics such as drugs use, sexuality, and violence in a calm and non-judgmental manner.

- let her know what you like about her and encourage her often.

Why Reward and Punishment Often Backfire

Autocratic parents often use reward and punishment as their primary tools for controlling their teens. This method is sometimes effective in an autocratic environment, but in a society of equals it usually makes matters worse. Here, when a person is rewarded for an achievement or behavior, that person eventually comes to expect the reward as a right every time he does the same thing. He begins to believe he is entitled to that reward, and he feels resentful if he does not get it.

The same is true for teens whose parents reward them for positive behavior. They get used to receiving a reward and eventually regard it as a right. Then they begin to develop a "what's in it for me?" attitude with little sense of the benefits of positive behavior or cooperation for the good of all. To make matters worse, if rewards are to continue to be

You and Your Partner: Support or Sabotage?

If you are a parent in a committed relationship, you may sometimes wonder what to do if you and your partner have different parenting styles. Of course, it's best if you both adopt an Active style of parenting, but when that is not possible, we recommend that you focus on your own relationship with your teen. Rather than using your new knowledge of Active Parenting skills to criticize or berate your partner, it's best to work towards supporting each other in spite of your differences. Also, avoid saying things to your teen that will undermine the other parent. Go over the following agreement with your partner and see if you can make it your own:

WE AGREE TO...

- put the best interests of our teen ahead of our differences.

- respect each other's right to see our teen's needs differently.

- discuss our differences in private—not in front of our teen.

- agree on how to handle situations together, compromising rather than bullying each other or giving in.

- present a united front to our teen, so that he is not tempted to split us.

- avoid undermining each other by criticizing the other parent to the teen, changing agreements without consulting each other, or otherwise trying to "score points" with our teen at the expense of the other.

- look for the positive in each other's parenting methods, and to encourage each other by pointing these positives out.

effective as incentives for positive behavior, parents must increase the value of the reward. When they reach their limits and get fed up, they often become angry and switch to punishment.

Though punishment can be effective in the short-run, it eventually leads to problems because it is based on the belief that you must hurt people in order to teach them. In a society based on equality, when a person is punished, that person often feels they have the right to hurt the punisher back. Punishing teens for misbehavior often leads them to resent their parents and to try to get even with them. It also doesn't teach teens how to behave responsibly or cooperatively, only how to avoid getting caught, how to make excuses, and how blame others.

All in all, reward and punishment as methods of discipline are holdovers from an earlier time when the world was a different place. Parents can employ much more effective methods of encouragement and discipline, methods we will be covering throughout this book.

Control versus Influence

We have all heard talk about how important it is for parents to control their teens. The truth is that the only person who can really *control* a teen's behavior is the teen himself. A parent's strength lies in *influencing* a teen's behavior and attitude. What's the difference?

<u>Control</u> means you have 100% power over the outcome.

<u>Influence</u> means you have between 1% and 99% power over the outcome.

If you tend towards the autocratic style of parenting, you probably try to over-control your teen. Ironically, sometimes the more control you try to exert, the more your teen rebels against your authority. If you tend towards a permissive style of parenting, you probably do not influence your teens enough. Either way, the result is that other influences, from peers to the media, gain the ground that you lose. If you are more of an Active parent, you work hard at being a positive influence in your teen's life, using a combination of respectful discipline and support. Even so, recognize that your influence can ultimately go only so far. Teens have free will and make the final decisions about their attitudes and behavior.

As important a role as we play in our teen's development, we can never take full credit or blame for the outcome. Many loving and effective parents have had teens make bad decisions and fail to thrive or even survive. On the other hand, many parents who were neglectful or abusive have had teens survive and thrive in spite of their negative influence. Parenting is really about probabilities. We improve the probability that our teens will succeed by being the best influence we can be and by encouraging them to be around other positive influences, as well.

Your Parent-Teen Relationship: Build it and they will come.

Most parents come to a parenting class or read a book about parenting in hopes of finding the magic bullet of discipline. It doesn't exist. There are certainly tricks you can use to modify your teen's behavior and bend him to your will, but these methods usually fall short in the long run. What works much better is a combination of solid discipline skills coupled with a strong relationship. A strong relationship increases your ability to influence your teen. Your ideas matter more. Your approval or disapproval matters more. Your rules matter more, and your discipline matters more. Build a strong relationship and your teens will more likely come around to your way of thinking about most things—not all things, because that would be counterproductive. After all, progress is only made when one generation improves upon the previous generation.

This book will provide you with many skills to help build your relationship with your teen, including:

- Mutual Respect
- Participation
- Problem Solving
- Family Enrichment
- Communication
- Encouragement

Let's take a look at the first two of these in this chapter and the others later.

Mutual Respect

Our teens are growing up in a society in which people are very sensitive to signs of disrespect. To disrespect somebody is often considered a personal affront—one that can even lead to violence.

Likewise, learning to respect oneself regardless of strengths, weaknesses, family, culture, or heritage is a building block for self-esteem and success. When you show your teen respect, even when you are angry or providing discipline, you help her learn to respect herself while demonstrating how to treat others respectfully.

"Respect is something you have to give in order to get."

– Bernard Malamud

In fact, treating your teen respectfully demonstrates how to treat *you* respectfully. As the author Bernard Malamud once wrote, "Respect is something you have to give in order to get." In other words, if we want someone to treat us respectfully, our children included, then we have to be willing to treat them respectfully, too. This concept of "mutual respect," as Rudolf Dreikurs called it, is often easier said than done. Showing teens respect means not yelling, cursing, calling them names, being sarcastic in a critical way, or otherwise speaking to them in ways you would not want them speaking to you. There are also countless more subtle forms of disrespect

to guard against. For example, an overprotective dad who is quick to jump in to solve his teenage daughter's problem—without giving her a chance to struggle to find a solution for herself—is being disrespectful. A mom who always insists on doing what she wants and never compromising to do what her teenage son wants is also showing disrespect.

When you catch yourself treating your teen disrespectfully, it is wise to smile, apologize, and if appropriate, make amends.

Examples:

"I'm sorry I yelled at you. That wasn't very respectful. Let me try again more calmly to tell you why I was angry."

"I apologize for not calling to tell you I would be late. How can I make it up to you?"

As you make this effort to treat your teen respectfully, insist that your teen show you respect, as well. This will probably require teaching on your part: teens may not always know how to be respectful, so help them along.

Examples:

> *"I don't talk to you that way. Please do not talk to me that way."*

> *"I don't talk to you that way and I will not tolerate you talking to me that way."*

> *"I want the two of you to stop right now. We don't talk to each other that way in our family."*

As we will see in Chapter 3, when your words alone are not enough to correct misbehavior, respectful discipline might be called for. One effective method is to use a logically connected consequence to help get your message through.

Examples:

> *"Either talk to me without yelling or go to your room."*

> *"Either share the remote without fighting or there will be no TV at all."*

> *"Either talk to me respectfully about not letting you watch an R rated movie or there will be no movies at all this week."*

The respect with which you treat your spouse or significant other, your extended family, your friends, and even strangers sets an example for your teen. When mutual respect is a cornerstone of your own interactions with people, your children come to adopt it almost without trying.

The Method of Choice

One of the most effective ways to strengthen the parent-teen relationship is to allow teens to participate in the family decision-making process. When people are empowered to make decisions, a lot of good things happen: their self-esteem rises; they feel better about the authority figure giving them the choice; they feel more responsible for the outcome; and they become better decision makers in the future. So many of the power struggles that plague many parent-teen relationships could be sidestepped if parents would provide teens with choices rather than give them orders.

Here's an example of a typical power struggle between parent and teen:

Parent: *Please end that video game and start your homework.*

Teen: *I'll do it later.*

Parent: *You need to do your homework. Now end the game and get started.*

Teen: *I don't see why I can't do it later.*

Parent: *That's what you always say, but it doesn't get done! Now get in there and start your homework now!*

Teen: *That's not fair!*

When teens feel that their parents are trying to control them, they often rebel. The resulting power struggle leaves both parent and teen frustrated and angry.

Now, let's see how giving the teen a simple choice can head off the power struggle. The choice should be within the limits that you think are reasonable for the situation. This is the heart of "freedom within limits," which is the hallmark of life in a democracy, as well as in the Active style of parenting.

Parent: *I think we need to set a regular time for you to do your homework; that way I won't be nagging you all the time.*

Teen: *Aw, mom…*

Parent: *Would you rather do it before dinner or after?*

Teen: *After, I guess.*

Parent: *Okay. Right after dinner, then.*

Teen: *Okay.*

Choice Is Power

When you give a teen a choice, you give her legitimate power. When you give her an order, she will have to rebel to gain power. As leader in the family, give your teens choices that are appropriate for their ages and levels of responsibility. Sometimes these choices might be simple either/or choices, as in the last example. Other times you might give open-ended choices.

Examples:

> *"Remember, you're going to cook dinner tomorrow. What would you like me to pick up at the grocery store when I'm there this afternoon?"*

> *"We want to visit Grandma pretty soon. What's a good weekend for you?"*

When you start thinking in terms of choices for your teen instead of dictating to him or giving in, you begin to move from power struggles to problem-solving. Finding solutions that are acceptable to both of you is also a good way to prepare your teen to be a good decision maker, an ability that will be critical when he is confronted with choices about drugs, sexuality, and violence.

One word of caution: Don't make everything a choice. Sometimes teens just want a clear but friendly decision from a parent.

Ethnic Identity Development

If your teen belongs to a minority ethnic group, she may grapple with emotions and awareness above and beyond the changes all teens experience.

When children are young, they are aware of simple racial differences—skin color, for example—but not of the significance society assigns to these differences. As they grow into teens and have more opportunities for social contact, they begin to observe, make comparisons, and evaluate society's fairness. Often this increasing awareness has a predictable set of stages:

Conforming: This is a naïve acceptance of the dominant culture's values. At this stage, an ethnic minority child or young teen may put down her own family's culture while idealizing the dominant culture.

Questioning/Thinking: The teen begins to wonder why some people accept the dominant culture without complaint. She shows a growing interest in her own cultural heritage.

Resisting: The teen shows interest and pride in her own culture while rejecting the dominant culture's values, resisting dominance by the cultural and political majority.

Awareness: Finally, the teen begins to think more critically about her own culture, while still maintaining pride. She accepts certain aspects of the dominant culture, even as she continues to resist conforming to the mainstream.

The journey from conforming to awareness is likely to be a rough one for your teen, and it may take a long time. You can gently guide her through the stages with support, understanding, and lots of discussion. Try to suspend your own judgment; it's essential that your teen develop her own opinions about these critical issues. Encourage her to learn about her ethnic history, and share with her the history of your family. Teens want to learn, and they need to know that parents care about their feelings. Your support, not your resistance, will help your teen through this challenging time.

Drugs, Sexuality, and Violence: Storms at Sea

On Saturday afternoon, thirteen-year-old David met up with some buddies to play basketball. On the way to the blacktop, one of them pulled out a brown paper bag, unscrewed the top of the bottle of 80 proof whiskey inside, and took a swig. Without a word he passed the bottle to the guy next to him, who took a swig. As the bottle moved from teen to teen, the pressure on David mounted. He didn't want to drink, but he didn't want to look like a kid either. And he didn't want to be left out of the group.

▲ ▲ ▲

At about the same time, fifteen-year-old Jenna was on her way to see a movie with some girlfriends, one of whom had just gotten her driver's license. Before they got out of the car, the driver pulled out a joint, lit it and took a hit, laughing about how she couldn't watch movies anymore without being stoned. As the joint slowly made its way to Jenna, she thought about all the anti-drug education she'd gotten from school, from her parents… But then again, even her dad smoked pot, so how dangerous could it be?

▲ ▲ ▲

At 11:30 on Saturday night, an unsupervised party, seventeen-year-old James had already drunk six beers and was well on the way to "getting totally wasted" for the third time this month. His girlfriend, Selena, was drinking almost as heavily and beginning to enjoy the attention of Joey, another guy at the party. James was furious. The next time Joey got up to refill his cup at the keg, James followed him outside. He knocked the cup out of Joey's hand and started yelling at him, making loud threats. Both boys were itching for a fight, but someone separated them before the first punch was thrown. Unsatisfied and still angry, James left the party and drove home with Selena, cursing and yelling at her for being "such a slut." Selena yelled back. As they pulled into her driveway, James slapped her hard across the face and told her to "shut up."

▲ ▲ ▲

At the same party, just after midnight, fifteen-year-old Dawn was losing her virginity in an upstairs bedroom with Keith, a boy she had known only a few weeks. Earlier, both had taken Ecstasy. Keith had told her that it made sex "amazing," and Dawn had pretended like she'd already had sex so that he wouldn't think she was scared or inexperienced. Dawn would later describe the experience as "nothing like I expected. It wasn't romantic at all and it hurt real bad. I was glad when it was over."

Do these scenarios shock you? Sadly, they are not extreme or even uncommon experiences among today's teens. Of all the challenges facing our teens, most parents would agree that the three most threatening are drugs, sexuality, and violence. Each of these dangers not only has the potential to damage a teen's life, it can also end that life. Many teenagers compound the risk factor by sailing into all three storms at once. As the stories above suggest, a teen high on alcohol or other drugs is many times more likely than a sober teen to become sexually active or physically violent.

Parents can do much to help prevent tragedy in these areas. First, the skills you learn in this book will help you build a positive relationship with your teen. This will increase your ability to influence your teen to make good decisions about drugs, sexuality, and violence. And when you offer choices instead of issuing commands, you empower your teen by letting him know that you trust him to make his own decisions. A good relationship based on mutual respect and trust decreases the likelihood that your teen will make bad decisions when you aren't there to guide him.

A good relationship based on mutual respect and trust decreases the likelihood that your teen will make bad decisions when you aren't there to guide him.

Second, by helping your teen develop courage, self-esteem, responsibility, cooperation, respect, and other important qualities, you help her achieve the stability of character, or ballast, needed to make it through the storms of adolescence and continue on to become a successful adult.

Third, you can use concrete prevention strategies to directly influence the chances of your teen becoming harmfully involved with alcohol and other drugs, sexuality, and violence. Later we'll present ten prevention strategies that are based on the findings of a task force I served on for the U.S. Office of Substance Abuse Prevention (OSAP)[1]. I have slightly modified these ten strategies to apply to sexuality and violence as well as drugs. These strategies will be presented in Chapters 5 and 6, building on the information and skills we'll be addressing in the first four chapters.

---

1   Now called CSAP (Center for Substance Abuse Prevention), which is part of SAMHSA (Substance Abuse and Mental Health Services Administration)

Family Enrichment Activity: Taking Time for Fun

Ever notice that a good salesperson will always spend time developing a positive relationship with you before she tries to sell you anything? She knows that half the job of effectively influencing a person is developing a positive relationship. Once the person has been "won over," the sale is much easier. (On the flip side, can you imagine a salesperson being autocratic and demanding a sale? "You'll buy this because I'm the salesperson and I said so!")

The more you can enrich your relationship with your teen, the more influence he will allow you to have in his life.

The same is true for parenting. The more you can enrich your relationship with your teen, the more influence he will allow you to have in his life. A positive relationship will prevent many problems as well as make discipline much easier when you need to use it.

At the end of each chapter we will present a family enrichment activity to help you strengthen your relationship with your teen. Your family enrichment activity for this chapter is to take the time to do something fun with your teen.

It's easier to like someone you have fun with. However, it's also easy to forget about the fun part of being a family when you're locked in conflict with your teenager or when your busy schedule doesn't leave much room for "quality family time." But fun may be exactly what your family needs! Enjoyable shared activities help break negative parent-teen cycles and enhance positive ones. The activity you choose can be brief (a ten-minute game of cards) or extended (a weekend-long outing). The key is to make it something your teen enjoys. For example:

- Throw a ball or shoot baskets.

- Prepare a fancy dessert together.

- Play a game together.

- Go on an outing (for example: hiking, a museum, a sports event, a festival).

To get the most out of this activity:

- Choose something that you both enjoy.

- Ask for suggestions from your teen, but have some ideas of your own.

- Keep it fun! Don't use this time for confrontation.

- Use the chart on page 37 to help plan the activity.

Use this family enrichment activity and the support skills you've learned on a regular basis and watch how your relationship with your teen blossoms. If your teen is frequently out of control, this may be a way to begin making positive contact. Be creative. And reach out.

Family Meeting: Choosing a Fun Family Activity

The Active Parenting model is designed to augment family life in a democratic society, where everyone may not get their way, but they always get their say. By holding family meetings, you can help prepare your children to survive and thrive in this society, teaching them the "give and take" that comes with cooperative problem solving and decision making. That is why we will present a family meeting at the end of each chapter.

We recommend that you use your first family meeting to decide what to do together for your family enrichment activity. Try to keep it informal and brief, and be careful not to turn this or any family meeting into a confrontation. This should be an enjoyable time during which everyone has his or her voice heard and their wishes considered. Stay upbeat and encouraging as much as possible and you will find that family meetings are a great benefit to parents and children alike—even teenagers.

chapter **1**

Home Activities

If you haven't started practicing what you've learned from this chapter with your family, then **now** is the time to put these ideas to work! You may feel a little unsure about your ability to use these new skills. Like most learning, the more you practice, the easier they will become. Begin by completing the following home activities. Some of them include a guide sheet on which you can plan or record your thoughts and experiences.

The sooner you start changing your behavior towards your teen, the sooner your teen will start changing her behavior towards you.

1. Reread any section from this chapter that you would like to be reminded about.

2. Think about your goals as a parent and what you hope to learn from this book. The questionnaire on page 34 will guide your thoughts.

3. Practice giving choices to your teen this week, and complete the Method of Choice guide sheet on page 35.

4. Make an effort to become more aware of how you and your teen show each other respect or disrespect this week. Fill out the questionnaire on page 36.

5. Have a family meeting to decide on a fun activity to do together. Then, as your family enrichment activity, do that activity. Help plan for the event by completing the guide sheet on page 37.

What I Hope to Learn

Think about your goals as the parent or caretaker of a teen. What do you hope to learn as you proceed through this book (or through the *Active Parenting of Teens* video-and-discussion program, if applicable)? This questionnaire will help you identify your goals.

1. What are your **strengths** as a parent? What do you do well?

generous

dedicated

loving

2. What are your **weaknesses** as a parent? What needs improvement?

patience   learning to pick & choose battles

temper

tend to fall back to mistakes my parents made

3. Write three things that you hope to learn from this book (or from this course):

1. Hope to learn more about how teens think

2. Hope to learn strategies for being a good parent + a more understanding parent

3. Hope to learn ways to bring peace during the ups + downs + how to maintain more ups + less downs

The Method of Choice

Use this chart to record the choices that you give your teen this week in an effort to empower her by encouraging her to participate in family decisions. After you have given each choice, write how it went.

CHOICES I'VE GIVEN MY TEEN:

Choice Given: _____

How did it go? _____

_____

Choice Given: _____

How did it go? _____

_____

Choice Given: _____

How did it go? _____

_____

Choice Given: _____

How did it go? _____

_____

Mutual Respect Questionnaire

Make an effort to be more aware of the concept of mutual respect this week, but only work on changing your own behavior right now. Answer the following questions on a daily basis, if possible, or as often as you can.

1. How have I acted **disrespectfully** towards my teen? _____

_____

_____

2. Did I catch myself about to act disrespectfully and change my behavior? _____

_____

3. How have I acted **respectfully** towards my teen this week? _____

_____

_____

4. Did my teen act disrespectfully towards me? How? _____

_____

_____

5. How did I respond to my teen's disrespectful behavior? _____

_____

6. What have I learned or relearned from this? _____

_____

_____

Family Meeting and Family Enrichment Activity: Taking Time for Fun

Remember when…

Describe something fun you did with your parents when you were a teenager. _____

_____

How did you feel about your parent at that moment? How did you feel about yourself? _____

_____

_____

Make a list of activities that you think would be fun to do with your teen. Add to the list as you discuss this topic at your family meeting. List the pros and cons of each activity.

Activity	Pros	Cons
1.		
2.		
3.		
4.		
5.		

Winning Cooperation

Tyra, fifteen, had the physical maturity of a grown woman and the emotions of a teenager. She really liked twenty-one-year-old Grant. He was good-looking, confident, and grown-up—not like the boys at school, who were just kids. Her mom, knowing that beautiful Tyra looked much older than her fifteen years, was worried. She repeatedly warned Tyra about getting involved with older guys, but Tyra dismissed her "nagging," and of course she didn't tell her mom how old Grant really was. *I can handle it,* she said to herself. *I'm more mature than other girls my age. Besides, Grant really likes me.* In reality Grant wasn't interested in having a fifteen-year-old girlfriend. He figured she would be easy, though, because she practically idolized him. It didn't take much to persuade her to have sex. Afterwards, Tyra was happy, thinking the physical intimacy meant Grant was committed to her. Little did she know then that he wouldn't even be around when the pregnancy test turned out positive. Now, alone and overwhelmed, she had no choice but to tell her mother. It was going to be the hardest thing she'd ever done.

▲ ▲ ▲

Ray, twelve, told himself this wasn't the end of the world, that lots of kids went through it these days. But when his dad had told him he was moving out, it was like the wind had been knocked out of him. How could his parents be getting a divorce? Sure, they fought a lot, but they had always assured him that things were OK. Now he'd be lucky to see his dad every two weeks. Suddenly, he hated everything about his life.

▲ ▲ ▲

Jenny, sixteen, was devastated. Being overweight had always bothered her, but she had managed to live with it. She had friends, and she was good in school. But nothing this bad had ever happened to her before. How could people be so cruel? Jenny recalled the incident with shame. She had been online, checking to see if her most recent post on a friend's web site had gotten any responses, when she saw it. There, under her comment, was a string of responses: "Jenny Franco is a fat cow!" "Moooo" "ROFL" "Someone tell that girl to get her fat *** on a diet." Of course, all the nasty posts were anonymous. She had no way of knowing who had written them—it could be anybody, even someone who acted nice to her in person! Jenny's friends told her not to let it bother her. "People will say anything on the Internet," they reassured her. But now she lay on her bed, staring at the ceiling and wondering what else people said about her behind her back.

Being a teenager is often painful. No one gets through it without some suffering. During the hard times, we can reach out to our teens and provide support. We can comfort, encourage, and help them use such problems to grow stronger. *Our role in such situations is not to discipline.* Tyra does not need a lecture on birth control at this moment, nor does she need to be grounded—both common parental tactics in this situation. She needs, first and foremost, the love and support of a caring parent. Ray doesn't need his dad to tell him to buck up and face his parents' divorce like a man; he needs a dad who is sympathetic and understands the pain his son is experiencing. And Jenny doesn't need a parent saying "I told you so" about her weight. Right now, she needs to know that she is loved and accepted as is. She needs an ally to help her face the cruelties of the world.

Supporting your teen when a storm like this hits can mean the difference between stability and growth on one hand or discouragement and failure on the other. Such a situation also presents an opportunity to teach the value of cooperation as you help your teen explore options for handling the problem. Cooperation, along with courage, responsibility, respect and self-esteem, is one of the five essential qualities that form the ballast of character that will help teens thrive in our democratic society. We define it as follows:

> *Cooperation:*
> *Two or more people working together in a mutually*
> *supportive manner toward a common goal*

A teen who learns to work cooperatively with others in solving problems has a far greater chance of success than a teen who stands alone.

The reason democratic societies flourish while those based on dictatorship or lawlessness flounder is in large measure due to the fact that *none of us is as smart as all of us.* When people work together cooperatively, problems are solved and civilizations are built. Likewise, a teen who learns to work cooperatively with others in solving problems has a far greater chance of success than a teen who stands alone. This chapter will explore communication as a support tool. We'll present parenting skills you can use to help your teen effectively handle her problems while strengthening your relationship with her in the process.

The Gift of Problems

Most people regard problems as, well, problematic. They figure that life would be better off without problems. But we can also think of problems as the motivation for most of our advances in life, both personal advances and those we see in the world around us. Let's face it: we humans can be pretty lazy. "If it ain't broke, don't fix it" becomes an excuse for maintaining the status quo—at least until it does break. Only then do we unleash the full power of our incredible ingenuity and imagination. Faced with problems, we develop cures for diseases, invent alternative fuel sources, grow more and better food, improve transportation, implement better systems of law and justice, and the list goes on and on and on. In fact, you could say that humans are the problem-solving species. It's what we do best, and when we do it we grow.

The difference between successful families and those that seem to endlessly struggle is not the presence or absence of problems. The difference is that some families are better at solving their problems, learning from the experience, and moving on.

Fortunately for us, there is no shortage of problems. The difference between successful families and those that seem to endlessly struggle is not the presence or absence of problems. The difference is that some families are better at solving their problems, learning from the experience, and moving on. The same is true for teenagers. All teens experience problems, which is a good thing. That doesn't mean we shouldn't work to prevent problems. Problem prevention provides a learning experience, too, and one that is often less costly. But despite our best efforts, problems will happen. A terrific kid will make a terrible choice or circumstances beyond anyone's control will bring bad things to good people. One way or another, we will all be gifted with the opportunity of problems.

To help you take advantage of these opportunities, much of this book is organized around the concept of handling problems. We will begin by looking at ways for parents and teens to build a cooperative relationship. Then we will explore how you can work together to solve the problems that teens own responsibility for handling. In later chapters we will include discipline skills that can help you solve behavior problems with your teens. Communication will be a key factor in both cases as we continue to stress the need for participation and mutual respect in handling problems successfully.

First, let's take a look at the Active Parenting Problem-Handling Model and examine the question of problem "ownership" to get an overview of how this all fits together.

Who Owns the Problem?

The first step in handling problems that occur with teens is to determine who "owns" the problem—that is, who should have responsibility for handling the problem. This step may be a more important part of solving a problem than you might first realize. Teens are very sensitive to their parents trying to run every aspect of their lives. Allowing them freedom to make decisions, even mistakes, when they own a problem is important in building a cooperative relationship. Dictators and Doormats tend to take on either too many or too few of their teens' problems. Active parents determine what to do by first determining who owns the problem:

Teens are very sensitive to their parents trying to run every aspect of their lives. Allowing them freedom to make decisions, even mistakes, when they own a problem is important in building a cooperative relationship

Parent-owned Problems: If the problem is due to the teen misbehaving, the parent as leader in the family owns responsibility for finding a solution. The discipline skills on the left side of the Problem-Handling Model can be used to find a solution in these cases. We'll address parent-owned problems in Chapter 3.

Teen-owned Problems: Teens encounter many problems that are not really their parents' responsibility. These problems are said to be owned by the teen. When they occur, a parent's job is to offer support using the skills listed on the right side of the model.

Shared Problems: Sometimes, problems are shared by the parent and the teen. In these cases, the parent can offer both support and discipline.

To help determine who owns a problem, ask yourself the following questions:

- Who is the problem behavior directly affecting? Whose needs or goals are being blocked? Who is raising the issue or making the complaint? That person usually owns the problem.

- Does the problem involve health, safety, or family rules or values? If so, then the problem belongs to the parent.

- Is the problem within reasonable limits for your child's age and level of maturity? If not, then either the parent owns responsibility for handling the problem or it is shared between the teen and the parent.

THE PROBLEM-HANDLING MODEL

Anticipate and prevent problems through problem-prevention talks and family meetings

If a problem does occur, determine who owns the problem:
(parent, teen, or both)

Parent-owned

Provide discipline.

Less-structured Discipline Approaches:
- Polite requests
- "I" messages
- Firm directions

More-structured Discipline Approaches:
- Logical Consequences
- FLAC method

Shared

Provide discipline and support.

Teen-owned

Provide support.

If appropriate, allow natural consequences to teach.

Let the teen handle the problem, but offer support through active communication.

Refer the problem to a family meeting

And no matter who owns the problem: encourage, encourage, encourage!

Let's look at some examples to help clarify this further.

Situation	Who owns the problem?	Why?
Teen drives the car into the garage too fast.	Parent	It's the parent's responsibility to teach a teen to drive safely.
Teen complains about her younger sister going into her room without getting permission.	Teen	Teen's goal of privacy is being blocked. Also, siblings need to learn to relate to each other on their own, without parents involved.
Teen forgets to do a household chore.	Parent	This affects everyone in the family, including the parents.
Teen doesn't come home until very late.	Parent	Parents have a responsibility to supervise their teens. This goal has been blocked by the teen's action.
Teen complains that her teacher gave her an unfair grade.	Teen	The teen, not the parent, is making the complaint of unfair grading, and it is reasonable to expect the teen to approach her teacher about it on her own.
Teen is not keeping up with schoolwork.	Shared	Although schoolwork is the teen's responsibility, parents have a right to get involved until the teen shows he is willing to handle this responsibility himself.

Let's summarize what we have learned about problems.

1. Problems can be learning experiences.

2. When a problem occurs, determine who owns it.

3. If the parent owns the problem, use discipline skills.

4. If the teen owns the problem, use support skills.

5. If the problem is shared, use discipline and support skills.

6. No matter who owns the problem, always look for opportunities to encourage, encourage, encourage.

Communication: The Road to Cooperation

Building a cooperative relationship with anyone requires effective communication. This is more challenging with teens because of the special circumstances of the teen years, such as:

- Self-esteem is often fragile during the teen years, so teens are quick to interpret what parents say as disrespectful.

- Because teens are trying to become independent adults, they often identify with their friends and not with parents. Most would rather communicate with a friend than a parent.

- Teens are busy experimenting with who they are in ways that parents may not approve of, from clothing choices to hair color to piercings. Arguments with your teen about these choices can keep you from communicating about deeper issues.

- Many teens feel that no one listens to them or cares what they think or how they feel. They often don't expect to be able to communicate with parents.

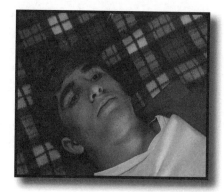

- Teens may be confused about who they are and what they stand for. Sometimes they just don't know what to say. They may not even know what they think.

Under all the funny hair and aloof attitude, this chameleon-like person is still your child, and she still wants your support and acceptance.

Despite these issues, many teens (according to one study, about forty percent) wish their parents spent more time with them. Under all the funny hair and aloof attitude, this chameleon-like person is still your child, and she still wants your support and acceptance. She may be pushing you away most of the time, but deep down she needs to hear from you more often.

Mixed Messages

Communication involves much more than just what you say to your teen. In fact, your message is carried on three separate channels:

Three Channels of Communication

1. **Your words**

2. **Your tone of voice**

3. **Your body language, including hand gestures, how close you stand, and facial expressions.**

When you communicate straight information, such as a shopping list, your words carry most of the message. However, with emotionally charged messages such as problems, research has shown that more of the message is carried by body language, followed by tone of voice and lastly, the words themselves. In other words, *how* you say something is often even more important than *what* you say.

When all three channels of communication carry the same message, the communication is very clear and powerful.

When all three channels of communication carry the same message, the communication is very clear and powerful. However, when you say one thing with your words and something else with your tone and/or body language, you send a *mixed message*. Mixed messages not only dilute the strength of the message, they often confuse the listener.

Imagine that your teen owns a problem and you've decided to let her handle it. You say, "You can do whatever you think is best." However, your tone of voice, crossed arms, and scowl all say, "I'll be very angry if you don't do what I think is best." This sort of mixed message makes it difficult for your teen to know where she really stands with you. The key to sending a clear message is to adjust your attitude so that you really accept your teen's right to make the decision without feeling angry. You may still be somewhat disappointed if she makes a particular choice, but you can change your words to more honestly reflect your feelings.

Example:

> *"I may be disappointed if you decide not to take your sister with you to the mall, but it's your choice. I can live with it." (Your face and tone need to say this, too.)*

If you give a mixed message while disciplining your teen, you are giving your teen an "out" because she'll probably listen only to the part of the message she wants to hear. It is much more powerful to give just one clear message.

For example, suppose you're busy in the kitchen when your teenage son comes in and asks you if he can go to a concert on a school night. You are preoccupied with cooking dinner, and when you respond to him, your words say one thing—"I don't think that's a very good idea"; but your tone says something different—"I'm not really that concerned. If you go ahead, that's your business. I don't care."

What do you think your teen will do? Since more of the message is carried through tone of voice, he's probably going to go to the concert. He might not even realize you don't want him to go. Remember this important principle of communication:

> ### *The clearer your communication,*
> ### *the stronger your message.*

Whether you're using discipline or supporting your teen in solving a problem, deliver a strong message by keeping your three channels of communication consistent.

Avoiding Communication Blocks

Most parents wish their teens would feel freer to come to them with their problems. Then we could help them solve these problems and eliminate the pain that such problems can bring. The trouble is that these very problems expose our children's self-esteem like a tender nerve. They may be extra sensitive to criticism, negative judgment, and other words or actions that seem to say that they are not worthwhile. These behaviors can block communication with the teen as effectively as a brick wall. If you are fortunate enough to engage your teen in talking about a problem, you need to guard against anything that might block communication and prompt her to withdraw.

> *A communication block is any words, tone of voice or body language that influences a person sharing a problem to end the communication.*

Because you communicate your attitude largely through tone of voice and body language, it is not enough just to watch your words. You have to adopt a supportive, non-judgmental attitude if you're really going to help. When you listen and respond with an attitude of support, your teen will begin to trust you with her feelings and share more of what is going on in her life. This sets the stage for you to influence her to make wise decisions. If you jump the gun and block communication, you will have lost this valuable opportunity to offer guidance and win cooperation.

The mistake parents often make is launching into an attempt to solve the teen's problem instead of offering empathy or encouragement.

Look at the list of common communication blocks on the next page. Each communication block in the left column represents a way that we may disregard our teens' thoughts and feelings and instead focus on controlling the situation. More often than not, these attempts backfire.

A teen in pain needs to know that someone else feels the pain with her. The mistake parents often make is launching into an attempt to solve the teen's problem instead of offering empathy or encouragement. Ironically, by trying to solve your teen's problems, you may actually diminish her self-esteem. Your goal should not be to take over and provide a solution or to take away your teen's pain; the goal should be to offer a caring ear, support, and encouragement, and to help your teen find a useful solution for herself.

The first step in learning to have a helpful discussion with your teen without blocking communication is to identify your most common communication blocks. Be honest with yourself! Once you are aware that you use them, be on guard the next time your teen has a problem, and work hard to avoid these pitfalls. When you find yourself using a communication block, catch yourself with a smile, apologize, and make a change.

Communication Blocks

Block	Example	Parent's Intention	What It Really Says to the Teen
Commanding	"What you should do is..." "Stop complaining!"	To control the situation; To provide quick solutions.	"You don't have the right to decide how to handle your own problems."
Giving Advice	"I've got a really good idea..." "Why don't you..."	To solve the problem for the teen.	"You don't have the good sense to come up with your own solutions."
Placating	"It isn't as bad as it seems" "Everything will be okay."	To take away the teen's pain; To make him feel better.	"You don't have a right to your feelings. You can't handle discomfort."
Interrogating	"What did you do to make him…"	To get to the bottom of the problem and find out what the teen did wrong.	"It's your fault. You must have messed up somewhere."
Distracting	"Let's not worry about that."	To protect the teen from the problem by changing the subject.	"I don't think you can stand the discomfort long enough to find a real solution."
Psychologizing	"Do you know why you said that?" "You're just being oversensitive."	To help prevent future problems by analyzing the teen's behavior and explaining his motives	"I know more about you than you know about yourself. Therefore, I'm superior to you."
Judging	"Why were you doing that in the first place?" "That wasn't a very smart thing to do."	To help the teen realize what she did wrong.	"You have poor judgment. You don't make good decisions."

Chart continued on the next page...

Communication Blocks (continued)

Block	Example	Parent's Intention	What It Really Says to the Teen
Being sarcastic	"Well, I guess that's just about the end of the world."	To show the teen how wrong her attitudes or behavior are by making her feel ridiculous.	"You are ridiculous."
Moralizing	"The right thing to do is..." "You really should..."	To show the teen the proper way to deal with the problem.	"I'll choose your values for you."
Being a Know-It-All	"Everybody knows that when something like this happens, you..."	To show the teen that he has a resource for handling any problem—you.	"I'm smarter and more competent than you are."
Focusing on Mistakes	"I don't think you should have said that."	To help the teen learn what she did wrong.	"There is more wrong with you than right."
Negative expectations	"Now, don't blow it this time." "I know you won't remember to..."	To get them to do the right thing with guilt or "reverse psychology."	"I have very little confidence in you." "Surely you couldn't get any worse."
Perfectionism	"If you had made all As you wouldn't have to worry about it."	To motivate the teen to do his best.	"You are never quite good enough."

The Heartbreak of Discouragement

From the French word *couer*, meaning "heart," courage is the strength at the heart of a teen's personality. It provides confidence to tackle life's problems, learn from setbacks, and keep trying when the going gets tough. We define it like this:

> *Courage is the confidence to take a known risk for a known purpose.*

Since all of life requires risk taking, courage is an essential foundation for teens to build character upon.

Since all of life requires risk taking, courage is an essential foundation for teens to build character upon. No wonder that the great psychiatrist Alfred Adler once said that if he had to give a child only one characteristic it would be courage. Over time, courage leads teens to positive behavior and success. Communication is one way that you can help your teen develop courage. We will talk more about how to build this vital characteristic in Chapter 4 when we focus on methods of encouragement.

But just as courage leads to positive behavior and success, its opposite, discouragement, leads to negative behavior and failure. Communication blocks not only obstruct communication between parent and teen; they also rob your teen of the courage she so desperately needs, leaving her *dis*-couraged.

As a parent, you are in a position to reduce the amount of discouragement you give your teen and to instead look for opportunities to encourage. When your teen sees that you have confidence in him, when you focus on his strengths and positive behavior, when you value him as he is—he feels encouraged to keep trying.

Active Communication

Instead of blocking communication and discouraging your teen, you can use Active Communication, a five-step process that will help you win your teen's cooperation and provide support. Active Communication works best when you want to work with your teen to help her solve a problem, whether it is a problem that she owns or one that you own together. There are five steps to Active Communication:

THE FIVE STEPS OF ACTIVE COMMUNICATION

1. Listen actively.

2. Listen for feelings.

3. Look for alternatives and evaluate consequences.

4. Offer encouragement

5. Follow up later.

---

1. Listen actively.

When you are listening actively, you do more than just receive information; you actively participate in the communication process. You listen with your eyes as well as your ears, keeping them focused on your teen. You listen with your intuition as well as your intellect, using all available brainpower to address the situation at hand. The goal of active listening is to encourage your teen to express what he is thinking and feeling. Here's how:

- **Give full attention.** Your teen may feel encouraged by the attention alone. It says, "I care about you. You matter. I'm here to help."

- **Keep your own talk to a minimum.** When your mouth is open, your ears don't work as well. So listen more, and talk less.

- **Acknowledge what you're hearing.** Let your teen know that you are taking her words to heart. You can say something as simple as "I see" now and then or even "Uh-huh." Ask questions to clarify, and after long stories give a quick summary to show that you are paying attention.

- **Listen with empathy.** *Empathy* means sharing another person's feelings. Try to feel some of what your teen is feeling, and show her with your tone of voice and facial expressions that you feel what she is saying. In short, listen to the feelings beneath your teen's words.

Examples:

> *"Tyra, you look like you just lost your best friend. What happened?"*

> *"Ray, this must be hard for you. Let's talk."*

> *"Oh, Jenny . . . That must have really hurt."*

2. Listen for feelings.

Your teen needs to acknowledge and accept his feelings rather than keep them bottled up. Often the repression of feelings eventually leads teens to have emotional or even violent outbursts, and many suffer from stress-related ailments such as stomachaches, headaches, and eating disorders, to name a few. Teach your teen to describe how he feels and then to reflect on his feelings before he decides what action to take. This is part of what is known as "emotional intelligence." People who learn to understand and manage their own emotions are better able to understand others' emotions. This aids them in all their relationships and provides a leg up when it comes to cooperating with others.

You can help strengthen your teen's emotional intelligence by listening for not just the content of the story, but also how he feels about it. Unless he comes right out and tells you what he's feeling, you will have to discover this yourself by listening closely to his tone of voice and watching his face, hands, and posture. By listening this way, you will not only pick up a great deal of information about your teen; you will also communicate to him the most powerful message of all: You care. Recent research on brain development suggests that this "feeling of being felt" by another is not only encouraging, but actually is instrumental in building important networks in the brain.

When you have an idea of what your teen is feeling, reflect those feelings back to him. You become what psychologist Haim Ginott called an "emotional mirror." Mirrors don't judge how we look or tell us what to do; they just reflect what is there. Reflect your teen's feelings and connect them to what happened—the "content."

Examples:

> *"This is a really scary situation for you, isn't it, Tyra?"*

> *"Ray, I know you are angry at me for being late."*

> *"You're worried about what the other kids really think about your weight, aren't you, Jenny?"*

When you correctly hit upon your teen's feeling, an interesting thing happens: your teen's head nods "yes," her eyes show recognition, and she continues talking. Your job at this point is to keep listening, empathizing, and reflecting back those feelings.

Examples:

"You sound really concerned about what to do about the baby, Tyra."

"I guess you're worried about what's going to go wrong next, Ray."

"Kids can be really cruel. I can see how it would make you angry, Jenny."

By reflecting feelings in tentative terms ("It sounds as though…"; "I guess…") you don't come across like you're trying to be a mind-reader or a know-it-all. If you miss your guess about what your teen is feeling, she can correct you. That way you're sure you understand what she is saying and feeling.

Example:

Tyra: *"No…. It's not that. I want to have the baby. I just can't believe he doesn't care anything for me."*

Mother: *"I see. You're really surprised he ran out on you that way."*

By adjusting to your teen's correction, the communication continues to flow.

Connecting Feelings to Content

WHAT THE TEEN SAYS	FEELING WORD	WHAT THE PARENT SAYS
"Mom, I'm not going to do John's dishes again!"	Angry	"You seem angry that I want you to clean all the dishes."
"I missed the foul shot, and we lost the game."	Disappointed	"That must be really disappointing for you."
"I hate the way I look in this uniform."	Embarrassed	"I guess you're embarrassed to wear it."

3. Look for alternatives and evaluate consequences.

Teens usually don't spend as much time developing and evaluating solutions to their problems as mature adults do. Until the executive part of the brain is fully developed, teens are likely to choose the first solution that occurs to them, without pausing to consider the pros and cons of their other options. A parent's role is to slow them down by helping them look at various options and predict the likely consequences of each.

When your teen owns a problem, begin by asking her such simple questions as:

> *"What can you do about that?"*

> *"What else could you try?"*

After each alternative that your teen comes up with, you can lead her to predict the consequences by asking:

> *"What do you think would happen if you did that?"*

It is best for your teen to think of alternatives on her own, without your prompting. This helps her develop her own problem-solving skills and the persistence to keep thinking when solutions do not come easily. It also keeps her from being able to blame you if a solution does not work out well, which strengthens her sense of responsibility. However, if your teen cannot think of solutions by herself, you can gently suggest some. Be very careful in these cases not to take over or otherwise seem to insist that she do it your way. Remember, she owns the problem, and your role is that of a helpful consultant who makes suggestions but does not dictate solutions. You might simply ask, "Would you like to know what others have done in a situation like this?"

The "Palms Up" Technique

When you help your teen come up with alternatives, it's a good time to use the **"palms up" technique**. By actually turning your palms up and saying, "I don't know what you will decide to do, but what if…," you can suggest an option while leaving the final decision in your teen's hands. This method lowers your teen's resistance and actually allows you to be more of an influence on her in the long run than if you pointed a finger and said, "Here's what you should do." In addition, by using a physical gesture and matching your words to your tone of voice, your message is carried very powerfully on all three channels.

Self-Disclosure

Another non-threatening way of introducing an alternative solution to your teen is through your own self-disclosure. If you faced a similar problem in your own life, you can share the story of how you solved it.

Example:

"That reminds me of a time when I wasn't invited to a party that I really wanted to go to. I sat around feeling hurt for awhile, but then I decided that I wasn't going to let the girl that was giving it ruin my whole day. So I called a friend of mine from another school and we spent the day together having a great time."

Be careful not to turn this into a lecture of the "when-I-was-child-I-walked-five-miles-through-the-snow" type. Remember, too, that your teen is free to use or not use your ideas as she thinks best. Unless her solution is unsafe or violates your family values, it's best for you to remain accepting even if she chooses an alternative that you think will fail. After all, she owns the problem. Plus, there is a lot to be learned from failed ideas.

4.   Offer encouragement

Once your teen has a potential solution to her problem, a word of encouragement from you can help give her the courage to put it into action.

Examples:

> *"That sounds like a good idea to me. Let's see how it works out."*
>
> *"I really like your attitude about this."*
>
> *"You are really thinking this through. Nice going!"*

5.   Follow up later.

You and your teen can gain a tremendous amount of insight by talking about how her problem turned out. First, ask your teen how she handled the problem. Then ask what results followed.

Examples:

> *"How did it go with…?"*
>
> *"Remember that talk we had about _____ the other day? I was wondering how it turned out."*

This follow-up helps your teen learn from the experience and validates that your interest was genuine. If the results were good, then a little encouragement from you is all that is required.

Example:

> *"That's great! I knew you could do it."*

However, if the results were poor and the problem still exists, or if new ones were created, then you can begin the Active Communication process over again to help your teen find another solution.

Putting Active Communication to Work

Now that you are aware of the five steps of the Active Communication process, look for opportunities to use them to help your teen solve her own problems. You'll find that the more supportive you are, the more cooperative your teen is likely to be.

If you find you are still fighting with your teen a lot, however, he may not be willing yet to sit down for a long discussion. You can still listen actively and listen for feelings. When you identify his feelings, express your empathy.

Examples:

> *"Boy, you sure look down."*
>
> *"I guess you're really ticked off."*
>
> *"That must have hurt."*

You can even use these skills when disciplining your teen or telling him he can't do something. It may help reduce his anger. Just having his feelings recognized and accepted can sometimes help.

Examples:

> *"I know you're angry that I won't let you go."*
>
> *"I'm sorry my decision feels so bad to you."*
>
> *"If looks could kill, I'd be in real trouble right now."*
>
> *"I can live with you not liking me very much right now, but I don't think I could live with myself if something terrible happened to you."*

Feeling Words

Although the English language has hundreds or even thousands of words that describe specific feelings, most people don't use many in their daily vocabulary. As you practice looking for the right words and metaphors to describe and mirror your teen's feelings, you'll find that your "feeling word" vocabulary increases and the job gets easier. To help with this process, we've included a list of feeling words for you to keep in mind.

PLEASANT Feelings		UNPLEASANT Feelings	
accepted	hopeful	afraid	jealous
adventurous	important	angry	let down
calm	joyful	anxious	lonely
caring	loving	ashamed	overwhelmed
cheerful	peaceful	defeated	rejected
comfortable	playful	disappointed	remorseful
confident	proud	embarrassed	resentful
eager	relieved	frustrated	suspicious
encouraged	secure	guilty	uncomfortable
free	successful	hopeless	unloved
glad	understood	hurt	unsure
happy	loved	impatient	worried
King of the world		Down in the dumps	
Like a million dollars		Got the blues	
A-OK		Like your best friend died	
Fit as a fiddle		Burned out	
On the right path		Out of sorts	

Family Meeting: Getting to Know Your Teen Better

When your children were young, there probably wasn't much about them that you didn't know, from their favorite flavor of ice cream to their dreams for the future. Now that they're teens or pre-teens, your knowledge might be out of date. While it's unlikely that your teen has become a dramatically different person since childhood, there's little doubt that he or she has changed. It's time that you got to know your teen better. Your family meeting for this chapter is designed to help you do just that, through a casual interview about his or her interests and activities. Asking about these subjects says that you're interested in your teen's life and you value her as a unique individual.

To make this meeting go as smoothly as possible, we've constructed some questions for you to use when you interview your teen, which you'll find on pages 70 and 71. First, fill out the answers for the Parent's Questions and ask your teen to answer the Teen's questions. Then set a time to conduct an interview with your teen, and go over your responses to compare how close (or not so close!) you were.

Family Enrichment Activity: Letter of Encouragement

I discovered a powerful method of encouragement many years ago as a young Sunday school teacher. At the end of the school year I decided to write each of my students a letter about the progress they had made during the year. As I wrote the letters, I found myself focusing only on the students' strengths and what I liked about them. The students politely accepted these "letters of encouragement," as we now call them, as they left for summer vacation.

I didn't think much more about these letters until four years later. I was at a reception when a woman approached me and introduced herself as the mother of one of my students from that Sunday school class. "That letter you wrote Alice," she said, "meant so much to her. You know, she still has it pinned to her bulletin board."

What I learned from that experience is that "putting it in writing" carries extra weight in our society, and that this is as true with encouragement as it is with anything else. In addition, when you write a letter of encouragement, your teen can refer to it in the future and rekindle the warm feelings it generated, just as Alice did.

This chapter's family enrichment activity is to write your teen a letter of encouragement. Keep these guidelines in mind as you do:

■ Write about an improvement, not necessarily an accomplishment. Be specific.

■ Write only truthful comments. Don't say your teen has improved when he hasn't.

■ Write what you appreciate or enjoy about your teen.

■ Include how your teen's behavior has been helpful to others.

Let's look at two examples. The first is for a young teen already feeling a sense of courage and success:

Dear Megan,

I want you to know how proud I am of you. Every day I am amazed at how many positive ways you're growing. You show you're responsible in the way you keep up with your schoolwork, and your grades reflect that effort. More important, you are learning so much about the world and how it works. I've even learned some myself from our conversations about what you're studying!

I also admire how much effort you've put into improving in softball. Your throwing is so much stronger than it was just last year, and you are making contact with the ball almost every time at bat now. I really enjoy coming to your games and never imagined that softball can be so exciting. But why not? Your team has one of my favorite all-time athletes: YOU!

One other thing that I've noticed is how patient you are with your younger brother. When I saw you helping him with his reading the other day, I thought how lucky he was to have you for a big sister. Then I thought how lucky we all are to have you in our family.

Oh, one more thing: I really, really love you.

Dad

The next example is for an older teen who is working his way out of a pattern of discouragement:

Dear Tomas,

I just wanted to let your know that I appreciate the effort you have been making at controlling your temper. You have not blown up in over two weeks! In fact, you have had some really good ideas for solving problems around here. For example, your suggestion that you could take your sister to her party and pick her up if you could use the car for some errands in between worked out for everyone.

I also wanted to tell you how much I admire the effort you are putting into your schoolwork lately. You have really kept to the study time we set up, and it is starting to pay off. It takes a lot of courage to try your best at something that is neither easy or fun, and I know you would rather spend the time with your friends. That is what makes your hard work so special.

Anyway, I just wanted you to know that I appreciate the effort. If I can do anything to help, let me know.

Love,
Mom

chapter **2**

Home Activities

If you haven't started practicing what you've learned from this chapter with your family, take the time to put these ideas to work now. The following activities will help you get started.

1. Re-read any parts of this chapter for which you may need refreshing.

2. Complete the Communication Blocks chart on page 65.

3. Practice recognizing the five steps of the Active Communication process by completing the activity on pages 66-67 .

4. Look for an opportunity to use Active Communication with your teen. Describe your experience on the guide sheet on page 68.

5. Hold a family meeting to get to know your teen better. Use the guide sheet on pages 70-71 to structure your meeting.

6. Write a letter of encouragement to your teen and then give it to him or her.

Who Owns the Problem? Video Practice

Video Scene	Who owns the problem?	Why?
Scene 1: Derrick comes home late for dinner.		
Scene 2: Alex and Miranda fight over the computer. Their mother intervenes.		
Scene 3: Matt and his father disagree about the content of Matt's web site.		
Scene 4: Erin breaks the necklace that her stepmother let her wear.		
My problem:		

This guide sheet refers to the Active Parenting of Teens *discussion program. If you are using this Parent's Guide independently and are interested in participating in a discussion group, check out our web site for information:*
www.ActiveParenting.com/ParentingTeens

Communication Blocks

We all use communication blocks from time to time. To catch ourselves before we block communication, it helps to know what our individual pitfalls are. Think about the communication blocks you tend to use most often. Write them under "block". Then indicate the situations that usually bring them out and what you see as your intention for using each block.

Block	Situation	Intention
Distracting	Daughter came in last place at the track meet.	To make her feel better so I'll feel better.

Active Communication Activity

Directions: **In the video script below,**

Circle the feeling words and efforts to empathize.   [Bracket] encouragement.

Underline alternatives and consequences.   ✓ Check off the follow-up.

Mother:	Hey. You seem pretty miserable. And you've never cut school before.
Abby:	Well I'm not going so don't even try.
Mother:	You sound pretty upset about it.
Abby:	You would be too.
Mother:	I see. What happened that's got you so upset?
Abby:	Nothing.
Mother:	Sometimes it helps to talk about it.
Abby:	I doubt it…and it's not going to change my mind about going.
Mother:	Well, I can't make you go, Abby. And I don't know what you'll decide to do, but I would like to talk to you about it.
Abby:	Well, Steve, he's a senior and the editor of the yearbook and I'm on the staff for the freshman class and he called this big meeting and started yelling about people missing deadlines and stuff and the only person he called out by name was me. And when I tried to tell him my excuse, he cut me off and said this wasn't day care and it wasn't his job to baby-sit freshmen.
Mother:	Oh, Abby…That must have really hurt.
Abby:	I wanted to crawl under a desk and die.
Mother:	Pretty embarrassing!
Abby:	Yeah. I've never been so humiliated. The rest of them thought it was just hilarious. There's no way I can go back there!
Mother:	I can see why you'd feel that way.
Abby:	You can?
Mother:	Sure. I can remember… Well, maybe I shouldn't tell you this…
Abby:	Come on! I told you…
Mother:	Okay, well …now I was already a senior, and I went to the movies with a date and we parked. All we did was kiss a little, but he told everyone I was really easy and implied we'd done a lot more…
Abby:	What a jerk.
Mother:	Believe me, I called him much worse, and I was incredibly embarrassed by the whole thing.

    Activity continued on the next page…

Abby: Well, what do you think I should do? I can't just call him a jerk. And I *have* missed some deadlines.

Mother: So, as your editor he has the right to expect you to handle your responsibilities.

Abby: I guess… but he didn't have to be such a show-off and embarrass me in front of everyone!

Mother: No, I agree. That was uncalled for. Well, let's look at your options. You can hang out here the rest of your life with your dad and me...

Abby: Ugh. No offense.

Mother: None taken. What else could you do?

Abby: I could just quit the yearbook. Write him a note or something.

Mother: You could quit. How would you feel if you did?

Abby: Like a quitter. There's no way I'm going to give him the satisfaction of making me quit.

Mother: Well that's one way of looking at it. Tell me something, is this Steve guy really a bad person or was he maybe just feeling the pressure of deadlines himself?

Abby: Both. He's yelled at other people before.

Mother: I see. Well, there's something you should know about the world of work. Some bosses are like that, and you have to decide whether it's worth it to work for them or go someplace else. Of course, when you miss deadlines, you can get fired, too,

Abby: Yeah, well I guess he isn't that bad. I mean he does compliment me on my work...sometimes.

Mother: What if you asked to talk to him and told him how you felt about what happened?

Abby: Well...

Mother: I know. It would take a lot of courage. But I've seen you stand up for yourself before, and you've done it without being offensive.

Abby: Well, I'll think about it.

Mother: Let me know how it goes.

—TIME LAPSE—

Mother: Hi, sweetie. How'd it go at school today? Did you talk with Steve?

Abby: Nah. I didn't have to. He sort of apologized to all of us for yelling the other day, and he said that we were all doing a good job.

Mother: Well, then. I'm glad it worked out for you.

Abby: Thanks.

This guide sheet refers to the Active Parenting of Teens *discussion program. If you are using this Parent's Guide independently and are interested in participating in a discussion group, check out our web site for information:*
www.ActiveParenting.com/ParentingTeens

Active Communication

After you've had a chance to practice your Active Communication skills with your teen this week, fill out the following evaluation to help you learn from the experience.

What was the situation or problem that you talked to your teen about? _____

_____

How did you approach your teen? _____

_____

List examples of the five steps of Active Communication you were able to use:

1. Listen actively. _____

   _____

2. Listen for feelings. _____

   _____

3. Look for alternatives and evaluate consequences. _____

   _____

4. Offer encouragement. _____

   _____

5. Follow up. _____

   _____

How did your teen respond? _____

_____

What did you like about the process and how you handled it? _____

_____

What will you do differently next time? _____

_____

Responding to Feelings Video Practice

Scene	Teen's Feeling	Parent's Response
1. Alex		
2. Jada		
3. Derrick		
4. Justin		
5. Julie		
6. Matt		
7. Miranda		

This guide sheet refers to the Active Parenting of Teens *discussion program. If you are using this Parent's Guide independently and are interested in participating in a discussion group, check out our web site for information:*
www.ActiveParenting.com/ParentingTeens

Family Meeting: Getting to Know Your Teen Better

Fill in your answers to the Parent's Questions and ask your teen to answer the Teen's Questions. Then set a time to interview your teen. Compare your answers and discuss them with your teen.

■ Keep the tone positive. Avoid judging your teen or making negative remarks about any of her answers.

■ If you have more than one teen, conduct separate interviews so that each receives your undivided attention.

■ Add some of your own questions, but avoid topics that are too heavy unless your teen brings one up.

Parent's Questions:

1. Who is your teen's best friend? _____

2. What is your teen good at (both in and out of school)? _____

_____

3. What does your teen worry about? _____

_____

4. What do you do that drives your teen crazy? _____

_____

5. What does <u>your teen</u> do that drives <u>you</u> crazy? _____

_____

6. How would your teen like to contribute to society as he grows older? _____

_____

_____

7. Add your own question: _____

   And answer it: _____

_____

Continued on the next page...

Teen's Questions:

1. Who is your best friend? _____

2. What are you good at (both in and out of school)? _____

_____

3. What do you worry about? _____

_____

4. What do your parents do that drives you crazy? _____

_____

5. What do <u>you</u> do that drives <u>your parents</u> crazy? _____

_____

6. How would you like to contribute to society as you grow older? _____

_____

_____

7. _____

_____

_____

Responsibility and Discipline

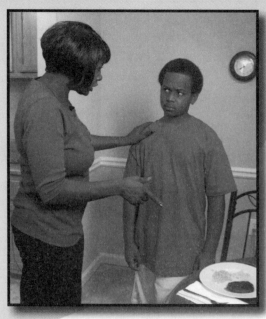

Karen, fifteen, liked a boy at school her parents were convinced was "bad news." He had not done anything wrong that her parents knew about, but his hairstyle and the way he dressed was enough to convince them that he was not suitable for their daughter. After he brought Karen home an hour after curfew one night, both of them with alcohol on their breath, Karen's parents forbade her to see him again. Karen protested that they were being unfair, and a shouting match began. Karen defiantly stormed out of the house, slamming the door behind her.

▲ ▲ ▲

Devon, thirteen, seemed to have no interest in doing the few jobs his mom had given him to help out around their apartment. She fussed at him about it, but she usually just gave up after a while and did them herself. It was easier than reminding him a dozen times, she figured. It bothered her if Devon's room remained for long in its messy state, especially when dirty dishes from the previous night's snacks were left lying around. But cleaning up after him was getting pretty annoying, especially since she worked full-time and was a single parent.

▲ ▲ ▲

Lisa, fourteen, had become a lot more interested in socializing than in schoolwork during the past year, and her grades showed it. Her parents were constantly on her case, but it did little good. Lisa would study for a few minutes then have to call a friend to talk over a question. This inevitably led to a long telephone conversation about anything but the original question. When her parents asked her about her grades, Lisa complained that school was boring.

What Is Responsibility?

Most parents would agree that the teens in the above situations are not behaving responsibly. But what does the term "responsible" really mean? For Active parents, the word means three things:

> ## Responsibility means:
>
> 1. Accepting your obligations
>
> 2. Knowing the difference between right and wrong, and doing the right thing as the situation calls for it
>
> 3. Accepting accountability for your actions

1.   Responsibility Means: Accepting Your Obligations

There are times in all of our lives when we would rather not do something we feel obligated to do. Responsible parenthood, for instance, is filled with times when we sacrifice our own immediate desires for the long-term benefit of our families. Helping your teen understand the need for occasional self-sacrifice is part of teaching them responsibility. When Devon's mother let him out of doing his chores, she missed an opportunity to teach him responsibility. The same is true when a parent lets a teenager out of going to a family wedding because the teen complains, "Why do I have to go?" In these situation, calmly explain to your teen that there are unwritten agreements between people called obligations. Fulfilling these obligations is part of what keeps relationships, and even communities and countries, strong. It's OK to acknowledge that sometimes fulfilling an obligation is not fun. In fact,

It's OK to acknowledge that sometimes fulfilling an obligation is not fun. In fact, that will help you empathize with your teen when he has to do it.

that will help you empathize with your teen when he has to do it. For instance, he might have to pass up an invitation to go to a party because he has a prior commitment to perform in a chorus presentation. You can let him know that it takes courage to pass up some of the fun stuff in life, but that it will pay off in the long run.

2. Responsibility Means: Doing the Right Thing as the Situation Calls for It

Helping our teens learn the difference between right and wrong is part of our jobs as parents. As teens earn the freedom to make decisions by themselves, they also take on the responsibility to determine what is right in any given situation. This is not always easy. For example, most adults would readily agree that it is right to obey the law, and that we should teach our teens to do so. Yet when Dr. Martin Luther King, Jr., broke the segregation laws of Alabama during the Civil Rights Movement, we recognized his actions as not only responsible, but also as moral and courageous. Over time, people came to discover that the laws were wrong and Dr. King was right.

Taking time to talk with teens about right and wrong in real-life situations is the best way to help them grapple with these difficult issues. Continuing to challenge your own beliefs as you expand your conceptions about right and wrong is also an act of responsibility and courage.

At the very core of responsibility is the idea that what happens to you results from decisions you make.

In the example of fifteen-year-old Karen, her parents had unfairly judged her boyfriend based on his looks. However, bringing their daughter home an hour late for curfew and drinking were other matters, and the parents had a responsibility to confront them about that behavior. Forbidding Karen from seeing her boyfriend again is not likely to be effective and will probably lead to more defiance. But this didn't make Karen's actions—storming out of the house—right either. Teens have an obligation to obey their parents in such situations, and leaving against their will was wrong.

3. Responsibility Means: Accepting Accountability for Your Actions

At the very core of responsibility is the idea that what happens to you results from decisions you make. Rather than accept this, it is much easier for people, including teens, to blame their problems on other people or circumstances, or just to make excuses. But laying blame and making excuses prevents them from learning to make better decisions in the future. After all, if it wasn't my fault, why should I think about what I could do differently next time?

For example, when Lisa's grades dropped because she was socializing too much and studying too little, she blamed it on her teachers for being boring. This thinking is not likely to help her improve her grades, since she can't control her teachers to make them more interesting. But what if she took responsibility and said to herself, "You know, there is a lot of boring stuff in those classes, but I want to do well in school, so I'd better study harder anyway. What can I do to make studying more fun?" When teens accept responsibility for what happens to them, they learn to prevent or solve their own problems.

You can think of responsibility as a formula:

$$R = C + C$$

Responsibility = Choice + Consequences

This formula covers all three aspects of responsibility, since "Choice" includes the choice to meet or not meet one's obligations and the choice of right or wrong.

How can you help your teen develop responsibility? First, recognize that teens often avoid responsibility because of how they're treated when they own up to their mistakes and misbehavior. Often their reward for taking responsibility is blame, discouragement, and sometimes punishment. Most people learn even as teens that if they can make a good excuse or blame it on someone else, they can avoid being hurt for their mistakes and misbehaviors. So, the first step in helping your teen learn responsibility is to avoid hurting her when she makes a bad choice. Try not to discourage her further through put-downs, punishments, or other disrespectful forms of discipline.

The first step in helping your teen learn responsibility is to avoid hurting her when she makes a bad choice.

To help your teen take responsibility without hurting her, you'll need discipline skills that are neither autocratic nor permissive. As we learned earlier, the Active style of parenting is based on the concept of "freedom within limits." This means allowing your teen the freedom to make choices within limits that are appropriate for her age and level of responsibility. The better your teen handles her freedom of choice, the more freedom you allow her in the future. It's time to talk in detail about these authoritative discipline skills.

Effective Discipline and the Problem-Handling Model

In Chapter 2, we discussed the importance of using problems as teaching tools for instilling qualities of character such as cooperation, courage, and responsibility in teens. We saw how using effective communication skills with teens can promote cooperation while helping them learn to solve problems. Let's take another look at the Problem-Handling Model that we presented in that chapter. Look at the model on the next page and notice that the left side has been highlighted. This side of the chart illustrates methods of handling *parent-owned* problems using effective discipline methods. But more important than just handling problems, these methods teach responsibility.

Effective discipline teaches responsibility.

The rest of this chapter explores how to use discipline skills to teach your teen responsibility and how to live within the limits that you determine as family leader.

When using any of the discipline skills that will follow, keep in mind these tips:

1. **Your goal is to teach your teens, not to hurt them.** In fact, the word *discipline* is derived from the Latin *disciplina*, meaning "teaching." And as school teachers and administrators learned a long time ago, we can teach far better without hurting our teens' feelings or their bodies.

2. **Whenever you discipline a teen for negative behavior, find opportunities to encourage any improvement the teen makes in the future.** Your encouragement will do a lot to promote more positive behavior. On the other hand, when a teen improves behavior after being disciplined and you ignore the improvement, it is very discouraging. After all, the teen unconsciously reasons, "If the only time I get noticed is when a mess up, why bother changing my ways? "

3. **When using discipline to influence your teen, use the least assertive method that works.** Research suggests that the less your teen attributes his positive behavior to outside forces (your discipline), the more he internalizes the reason for his positive behavior as his own. This leads him to form positive values which will promote positive behavior even when you aren't around to offer discipline.

THE PROBLEM-HANDLING MODEL

Anticipate and prevent problems through problem-prevention talks and family meetings

If a problem does occur, determine who owns the problem:
(parent, teen, or both)

Parent-owned

Shared

Teen-owned

**Provide
discipline.**

**Provide discipline
and support.**

**Provide
support.**

*Less-structured
Discipline Approaches:*
- Polite requests
- "I" messages
- Firm directions

*More-structured
Discipline Approaches:*
- Logical Consequences
- FLAC method

If appropriate, allow natural
consequences to teach.

Let the teen handle the
problem, but offer
support through active
communication.

Refer the problem to a family meeting

And no matter who owns the problem: encourage, encourage, encourage!

4. **Always explain the reason for the change in behavior you want.** Talking with your teen about the reasons for discipline will strengthen its underlying value. If you rely on the old saw, "Because I'm the parent and I said so!" you'd better be prepared to be around whenever your teen has to make a choice of right or wrong, because you're teaching her to do what she's told, not to do what is right. For your teen to learn values that will transfer to independent living, you have to explain the "whys" of your decisions.

5. **Let discipline be motivated by caring.** When your teen knows that you're disciplining him because you care, it's easier for him to accept. When you discipline out of frustration, anger, and your own personal goals, it's difficult for your teen to accept or learn the lesson you're trying to teach.

6. **Keep the focus on the problem, not the teen.** This keeps the discipline from getting personal, which tends to set off angry feelings and leads to power struggles and retaliation. For example:

    NOT: *"Honestly, you are so lazy!"*

    BETTER: *"We need to come up with a better plan for getting your homework done."*

7. **Invite your teen's participation.** Remembering what you've learned about freedom of speech and the importance of participation in a democratic society, be sure to involve your teen in the problem–solving process. For example:

    BEST: *"We need to come up with a better plan for getting your homework done. What do you suggest?"*

8. **Stay respectful.** Discipline that is disrespectful of your teen will make most problems worse and damage your relationship.

Basic Discipline Methods

The first three discipline methods we'll present are basic communication methods that increase in assertiveness from mild to firm. Start with the first, and if it doesn't work, move on to the second and then the third. They are:

- Polite Requests
- "I" Messages
- Firm Reminders

Polite Requests

Not every problem or conflict requires firm discipline or a lot of discussion. Asking your teen politely for what you want is often enough to influence him to change his behavior.

Not every problem or conflict requires firm discipline or a lot of discussion. Asking your teen politely for what you want is often enough to influence him to change his behavior, especially if your relationship is already a positive one.

When your teen doesn't know what you want in a situation, your first step is to politely make your desires known through a request. For example, you have decided that you no longer want to pamper your teen by picking up the dirty dishes he leaves in the den. Your polite request might be, "Honey, from now on will you do me a favor and bring your dirty dishes to the sink when you're through with your snack?" If your teen agrees, be sure to add, "Thanks. That will be a big help."

This may seem so simple that it sounds ridiculous, but sometimes that's all teens need. Of course, you could wait until you're fed up with being a servant, let it simmer inside for another week until it starts to boil, then burst out with, "I'm

sick and tired of having to pick up your mess! What do you think I am, your servant? If you weren't so lazy and inconsiderate…" However, this is not likely to produce responsibility, cooperation, or dishes in the sink.

If at first your teen does not comply with your polite request, offer a friendly reminder: "Honey, I noticed you forgot to put your dishes in the sink. Please come get them."

"I" Messages

If your teenager repeatedly forgets to keep an agreement or continues the problem behavior, you'll need a stronger message. "I" messages are a firm and friendly communication method that can produce surprisingly effective results. Psychologist Tom Gordon called them "I" messages in his pioneering program, *Parent Effectiveness Training* (P.E.T.), because they shift the emphasis from the teen (a traditional "you" message) to how the parent ("I") feels about the teen's behavior.

"I" messages:

- allow you to say how you feel about your teen's behavior without blaming or labeling her.

- create a situation in which your teen is more likely to hear what you are saying because you say it in a respectful manner.

- tell your teen how her behavior affects others (your feelings).

- put the emphasis on your teen's behavior rather than his personality.

- give your teen clear information about what change in behavior you want.

When to Use an "I" Message

Since "I" messages work best when delivered in a firm, calm tone of voice, avoid using them when you are too angry.

"I" messages are effective only when the parent owns the problem—when you have the responsibility and authority to decide on the solution. Since "I" messages work best when delivered in a firm, calm tone of voice, avoid using them when you are too angry. Allow time to cool off, then approach your teen when you have regained control. An angry "I" message can easily trigger rebellion in a power-seeking teen.

How to Send an "I" Message

There are four parts to an "I" Message:

1. **Name the behavior or situation you want changed.** In order to avoid attacking your teen's self esteem, it's important to "separate the deed from the doer." It isn't that your teen is bad, only that you have a problem with something he is doing. By beginning with a statement aimed at the behavior, you avoid attacking his personality and self-esteem. You begin with, "I have a problem with..."

Example:

"I have a problem with your leaving dirty dishes in the den."

2. **Say how you feel about the situation …**and say it without raising your voice. This lets your teen know that the problem is serious to you. Although parents often use the word "angry" to describe their feelings, this frequently masks other emotions, mainly fear and hurt. Teens are able to hear us better when we use feeling words to describe our real feelings because it's less threatening. "I feel concerned" or "I feel hurt" may be both closer to the truth and more effective than "I'm angry." So, this part of the "I" message begins with "I feel..."

Example:

"I feel taken advantage of... "

3. **State your reason.** Nobody likes to be treated as if he were expected to be blindly obedient. If you're going to change what's comfortable to you to please an authority, you at least want that authority to have a good reason for asking you to make the change. Teenagers feel this just as strongly as adults do. A simple explanation about how your teen's behavior is interfering with your needs or the needs of the situation can go a long way.

Example:

"…because I have to spend time and energy cleaning up after you."

4. **Say what you want done.** You've already made a polite request or two, so now you're getting more assertive. This means letting the teen know exactly what you'd like done. Remember, you get more of what you ask for than what you don't ask for. This step can begin with "I want" or "I would like."

Example:

"When you leave the den, I want you to bring your dirty dishes to the kitchen and put them in the dishwasher."

Putting this "I" message all together, we have:

> *"I have a problem with your leaving dirty dishes in the den. I feel taken advantage of because I have to spend time and energy cleaning up after you. When you leave the den, I want you to bring your dirty dishes to the kitchen and put them in the dishwasher."*

Making "I" Messages Stronger: Two Variations

1. **Getting agreement.** *"Will you please . . ."*
   You can make an "I" message even stronger by getting an agreement from your teen about the behavior you want changed. This can be done by simply adding the question, "Will you do that?" and then not moving until you get a "yes." Eye contact strengthens it more. Saying "yes" also verbally commits the teen to action and helps motivate her to follow through later. This can also be done by changing the last step of the "I" message from "I would like . . ." to "Will you please . . ."

   Example:

   > *"I have a problem with your leaving dirty dishes in the den. I feel taken advantage of because I have to spend time and energy cleaning up after you. Will you please bring your dirty dishes to the kitchen and put them in the dishwasher when you are finished? Will you do that?"*

2. **Establishing a time frame.** *"When?"*
   Every parent knows the frustrations of getting an agreement from a teen about doing something, finding it still undone hours later, and confronting the teen only to hear the refrain, "I'll do it." The implication, of course, is "I'll do it when I get around to it," and that may not occur in this decade. Your solution is to get a clear agreement as to when the behavior will be completed. In the above example, the "when" is built into the phrase "when you're finished?" Other times, it can be added right after the teen agrees to the request by simply asking, "When?"

Firm Reminders

Changing habits is not easy. Your teen has gotten used to whatever behavior you are trying to change, and even with good intentions, he will probably sometimes forget. Other times he may test to see if you are really committed to the change by sliding back into the old negative behavior. In either case, your next step is to give a short but firm reminder. By suspending the rules of grammar and syntax, you give the message additional "oomph."

Example:

"Dishes. Sink. Now."

The fewer words you use, the better. This means avoiding the temptation to give a lecture on responsibility while your teen sits there ignoring you. Just make solid eye contact and firmly remind your teen about what you want done—and when.

Your teen may very well spring into action, amazing you and surprising himself in the process. If so, build on this success, as always, by encouraging him with a thank-you. But even if he is less than enthusiastic, focus on his positive behavior at this point, and not his negative attitude.

Example:

NOT THIS:

Parent: *"Dishes, Sink. Now."*

Teen: *"Whatever."* *(Said as he slowly gets up and slouches towards the kitchen, dirty dishes in hand.)*

Parent: *"WHAT'S YOUR PROBLEM?! I DON'T SEE WHY YOU CAN'T DO A SIMPLE THING LIKE PUTTING YOUR *&%*$ DISHES IN THE SINK WITHOUT MAKING A HUGE DEAL ABOUT IT! IS THAT TOO MUCH TO ASK? I THINK NOT!"*

THIS:

Parent: *"Dishes. Sink. Now."*

Teen: *"Whatever." (Said as he slowly gets up and slouches towards the kitchen, dirty dishes in hand.)*

Parent: *"Thanks. I appreciate it."*

Your encouragement may eventually help your teen change his attitude to match his behavior. So, keep it positive.

Some kids seem to need a lot of reminders, in which case it may be time to move on to the more advanced discipline methods: the rack and the screw. (Just kidding! These medieval methods have been replaced in this edition with logical consequences and the FLAC Method.)

Advanced Discipline Methods

When basic discipline methods do not solve a problem that you own, you can turn to more advanced skills:

- Natural and Logical Consequences
- The FLAC Method

Natural Consequences

Remember that a key aspect of responsibility is accepting that what happens to us is a result of our choices.

Teens learn a lot about what works and what doesn't from the consequences of their actions.

Responsibility = Choice + Consequences

It stands to reason, then, that to teach your teen responsibility for her actions, you must give her the freedom to make choices and let her experience the consequences of those choices. Teens learn a lot about what works and what doesn't from the consequences of their actions. There are two basic types of consequences: natural and logical.

As the concept of "natural consequences" applies to parenting teens, we define it as follows:

> ## NATURAL CONSEQUENCES:
> ### *The results that occur from a teen's behavior*
> ### *without any interference by a parent*

Examples:

- *The natural consequence of not putting gas in the car is running out of gas.*

- *The natural consequence of oversleeping on a school day is being late for school.*

- *The natural consequence of leaving a bicycle outside may be that it gets rusty or that it is stolen.*

Natural consequences are powerful teachers. We have all learned important life lessons from the consequences of our own direct experience without parents or others intervening in any way. Natural consequences work well with teenagers because they allow the parents to act as a sympathetic third party rather than the disciplinarian. In order for natural consequences to be effective, avoid two temptations:

1. Don't rescue your teen on a regular basis from the natural consequences of his actions.

2. Don't say "I told you so" or otherwise lecture your teen on her mistake. It's better to say, "Gee, honey, I know that's frustrating." Then let the natural consequence do their teaching.

When You Can't Use Natural Consequences to Teach

There are three circumstances in which a responsible parent cannot allow Mother Nature to take her toll:

1. **When the natural consequence may be dangerous.** For example, the natural consequence of experimenting with drugs can be addiction or even death.

2. **When the natural consequence is so far in the future that the teen is not concerned about it.** For example, the natural consequence of not doing school work may be not graduating, not getting into one's college of choice, or fewer career options.

3. **When the natural consequence of a teen's behavior affects someone other than the teen.** For example, your teen returns your car with the gas gauge on empty, and you run out of gas. In such a situation, the parent owns the problem and must take action to prevent such natural consequences from occurring. In this case, allowing a natural consequence may not be your best discipline choice.

Logical Consequences

In cases in which you cannot rely on natural consequences, you'll need to set your own consequences. The consequence that you set needs to be logically related to your teen's misbehavior in order to teach your teen responsibility. For this reason, we call these "logical" consequences.

> *LOGICAL CONSEQUENCES:*
> *Discipline that is logically connected to a misbehavior and is applied by an authority to influence a teen to behave within the limits of the situation*

Examples:

- *When Sean continually forgets to bring his dirty dishes into the kitchen after snacking in the den, he loses the privilege of taking food out of the kitchen.*

- *When Susan forgets to put gas in Mom's car when she borrows it, she is not allowed to use the car for a week.*

Logical consequences are not the same thing as punishment, even though the teen won't like either. Some of the differences are:

LOGICAL CONSEQUENCES	PUNISHMENT
logically connected to the misbehavior	arbitrary retaliation for misbehavior
intended to teach responsibility	intended to teach obedience
given in a firm and calm way	often delivered with anger and resentment
respectful	disrespectful
allow the teen to participate	dictated by authority

How to Use Logical Consequences

Many parents unintentionally turn a would-be logical consequence into a punishment, and then they wonder why their teen responds with anger, rebellion, or a power struggle. To be sure you're giving a logical consequence and not a punishment, follow these guidelines. They may seem like a lot to remember at first, but as you practice, they'll become second nature.

GUIDELINES FOR USING LOGICAL CONSEQUENCES

1. Ask your teen to help decide the consequence.

2. Put the consequence in the form of a choice:
   either/or choice   when/then choice

3. Make sure the consequence is logically connected to the misbehavior.

4. Give choices you can live with.

5. Keep your tone of voice firm and calm.

6. Give the choice one time, then enforce the consequence.

7. Expect testing (it may get worse before it gets better).

8. Allow your teen to try again after experiencing the consequence.

1. Ask your teen to help decide the consequence.

Since the Active style of parenting is based on respect and participation, it is wise to ask your teen to help in deciding the consequences of her misbehavior. You stand a much better chance that your teen will cooperate with you if you include her in the decision-making process. You might be surprised how often she comes up with choices and solutions that you wouldn't have thought of on your own. On the other hand, teens will sometimes respond with typical punishments (grounding, push-ups, and the like.) So, you'll need to explain that the concept of logical consequences is a tool to help them learn, not a punishment to make them sorry.

You might be surprised how often your teen comes up with choices and solutions that you wouldn't have thought of on your own.

Example:

> *"Katherine, I still have a problem with you leaving your things all over the den. What do you think we can do to teach you to stop doing this?"*

Even if your teen gives you no helpful suggestions or is uncooperative about finding a solution, it is important that you asked. Since you have invited the teen's participation, she will be less likely to think of you as a dictator and to rebel against the consequence.

2. Put the consequence in the form of a choice.

Logical consequences teach responsibility, which means "choices plus consequences"; therefore, always present your logical consequence in the form of a choice. Your teen can choose positive behavior with a naturally occurring positive consequence, or she can choose to misbehave and have you provide a logical consequence.

Try one of these types of choices:

- *Either/or choices: "Either _____ or _____ . You decide."*

- *When/then choices: "When you have _____, then you may _____."*

Either/or choices are best used when you want to influence your teen to stop a behavior. Remember to follow the eight guidelines of logical consequences. Examples of either-or choices:

Katherine leaves her stuff scattered around the den in the afternoon.

YES: *"Katherine, either put your things away when you come home from school, or I'll put them in a box in the basement. You decide."*

NO: *"Katherine, put your things away or I'm going to throw them in a box in the basement!"*
(This choice makes the parent sound like an angry dictator.)

Harper regularly comes home twenty or thirty minutes past her curfew.

YES: *"Harper, either get yourself home at the time we agreed on, or we'll set your curfew earlier. You decide."*

NO: *"Harper, either start coming home on time, or you'll be sorry."*
(This is a threat, not a choice.)

When/then choices are best used when you want to influence your teen to start a positive behavior. They take two events that occur already and order them so that the teen must do what she likes doing less before she is allowed to do what she prefers. This is not a bribe or reward, because both behaviors are normal part of the teen's life already. Examples of when-then choices:

Selina has trouble getting her homework done but likes to surf the Internet.

YES: *"Selina, when you have finished your homework, then you may get on the Internet."*

NO: *"Selina, if you do your homework, you may use the computer an hour longer than usual tonight."*
(This is a reward, not a logical consequence, because it offers the teen something extra for something she should be doing anyway.)

Tom is about to go to the swimming pool, but he has ignored his regular Saturday chore of mowing the lawn.

YES: *"Tom, when you've mowed the lawn, then you may go swimming."*

NO: *"Tom, you may not go swimming until you have mowed the lawn."*
(That doesn't sound like a choice.)

3. Make sure the consequences are really logical

No matter who comes up with the consequence, it won't work unless it is logically connected to the misbehavior. Your teen will be better able to see the justice of such consequences and more likely to accept them without resentment. If the consequence is not really related to the teen's behavior, however, it is just another punishment.

NOT LOGICAL	LOGICAL
"Either be home by six o'clock or lose the privilege of watching TV for a week."	"Dinner is served at seven o'clock. Either be here on time or eat it cold, but at 7:30 we're clearing the table."
"Either share the computer with your brother or you're not going out on Saturday."	"Either share the computer with your brother or neither of you will be able to use it tonight."
"Finish your homework or you're grounded."	"When you finish your homework each weekday, you can go out that weekend." *

* This is logical if you establish a "work before play" philosophy in your family.

Tip: There are many logical consequences that will work for any given problem, but thinking of them does not always come easily, especially if you're accustomed to using a few basic punishments like grounding for every problem. With practice, logical consequences will begin to come to you more easily. It will help to brainstorm logical consequences for specific problems with your partner, a close friend, or with other parents and a leader in an *Active Parenting of Teens* group.

4. Give choices you can live with.

Regardless of where the logical consequence originates, if you own the problem, it's up to you to be sure the consequence is not only logical but also is one you can accept. If you are not comfortable with the consequence, it probably won't be effective with your teen.

For example, if your teen continually forgets to put his dishes in the dishwasher, a choice might be: "Either put your dishes in the dishwasher, or I will let them sit in the sink until you do." However, if you know that a sink full of dirty dishes will drive you crazy and make you angry at your teen, think of another option. You might get creative: "Either put your dirty dishes in the dishwasher, or when we run out of clean dishes, I'll serve dinner without them!" Although a dinner of spaghetti and meatballs served on a bare table would certainly make an impression on your teens, not many parents would be comfortable with that consequence. Try a different angle: "Either put your dishes in the dishwasher, or anyone else in the family can do your job and you can pay them to do it." As you can see, there are as many possible logical consequences as you can think of, so be creative and patient, and do what feels right for you.

5. Keep your voice firm and calm.

When you give a choice, and later when you enforce the consequence, it's important that you remain calm and use a firm tone of voice. An angry tone of voice (the autocratic parent's pitfall) invites rebellion and a fight. At the other end of the spectrum, a wishy-washy tone of voice (the permissive parent's pitfall) tells your teen that you don't really mean what you say, which also invites rebellion. A firm and calm tone by an authority figure says, "I will treat you respectfully, but you are out of bounds here. My job is to help you learn to stay in bounds, and I plan to do my job."

6. Give the choice one time, then act.

For a logical consequence to be effective, you must enforce it. If, after you give your teen a choice, he continues the problem behavior, immediately follow through with the consequence. Do not give the choice a second time without putting the consequence into effect. Your teen must see that his choice results in a consequence. More importantly, your teen must see that you mean what you say. You don't want to be harsh about it, but you do want to consistently enforce the consequence.

Example:

Michael's parents gave him a choice: either leave any party at which alcohol or other drugs are present, or lose the privilege of going to parties for a month. One night while Michael was at a party, his parents called the hosting parents to see how it was going. They were alarmed to learn that some teens had been caught sneaking alcohol in and were sent home. The host parents also shared their suspicion that others probably had done the same thing but hadn't gotten caught. When Michael got home, his parents subtly checked for signs of alcohol use. He appeared normal, so they asked him if he knew about the drinking at the party. He confessed that he did but that he hadn't drunk any himself.

"We appreciate that you showed the good judgment not to drink," Michael's mother said. "But since we agreed that you would leave parties that had alcohol or drugs, and you chose to stay, you won't be able to go to any more parties for a month."

"That's not fair!" Michael complained. "I did nothing wrong!"

"Let's remember why we set this consequence in the first place," his father replied calmly. "It's because any party where people are drinking or using drugs can get out of control quickly, and people can get hurt whether they are sober or not. And I'll also remind you that all of us agreed on these terms."

Although Michael was not happy, he knew his parents were right. He had known that by staying at the party he was challenging their agreement, but he'd assumed they wouldn't follow through with the consequence. Now he realized he should take his parents and their consequences more seriously.

7. Expect testing.

When you begin to set consequences to influence your teen towards making positive choices, expect her to continue to misbehave for a while. In fact, expect that it may get worse before it gets better. Like Michael in the above example, your teen is testing you to see how firm your limits really are and if you will really do what you say you will do. If you consistently enforce the consequences you set, in time she will see that her testing isn't weakening you, and she'll improve her behavior. After all, teens don't do what doesn't work. But until then, don't get overly angry when your teen tests you—because they almost always will. Just continue enforcing the consequence firmly and calmly.

Tip: In some cases you might observe that your consequence just doesn't matter much to your teen. This isn't testing; it's a form of teenage "deal

If you suspect that your teen is not motivated by the consequence you have set, then you'll either need to find a different one or attack the problem in other ways.

making." For example, when Jared hits his little brother, his mother enforces the logical consequence of sending him to his room for an hour. She reasons that this is a logical consequence because if Jared can't be around other people without hitting, then he shouldn't be around other people for a while. But while he's in his room, Jared thinks, *"Being in my room isn't so bad. I have my computer, my video games, my telephone—everything I need. Plus, that kid really gets on my nerves, and he deserved a good smack. All in all, I'd say the price was well worth it."* If you suspect that your teen is not motivated by the consequence you have set, then you'll either need to find a different one or attack the problem in other ways: a family meeting or the FLAC method (covered in the next section of this chapter.)

8. **Allow your teen to try again later.**

Since you want your teen to learn from the consequences of his choice, you need to give him a chance to try again after he's experienced the logical consequence.

Example:

Sondra has agreed to do her chores on Saturday before going off with her friends. Saturday afternoon, her dad notices that she has gone without doing them. When she comes home he tells her: "I noticed that you didn't do your chores before you left today as we agreed. That means you'll be staying home all day tomorrow to do them. You can try again next Saturday." The following weekend, Sondra leaves again without doing her chores. Dad tells her: "I think you'd better plan on spending next weekend at home, Sondra." (Notice that the length of time before the teen gets to try again gets longer with each misbehavior.)

The FLAC Method

As I mentioned earlier, my wife and I are ourselves parents of teens, and the skills in this book have been well used in our household. However, we rarely need to use logical consequences to solve a problem. When I take a closer look at what we're doing instead, I find that one of our most common approaches to problem-solving is not one skill but a combination of four. Individually, these skills are useful; combined, they are a powerful way solve problems cooperatively and to head off angry power struggles before they occur. I coined the acronym FLAC to help parents remember the four steps of this method, because it helps reduce the "flack" that power struggles often cause. The letters stand for:

Feelings

Limits

Alternatives

Consequences

Let's review the four steps:

FEELINGS. You saw in Chapter 2 how important it is to listen and respond to your teen's feelings. When you show empathy in this way, a teen who previously saw you as her enemy starts thinking of you as an ally. By acknowledging her feelings, you encourage the understanding that the two of you are working together to find a solution to a common problem. This goes a long way towards defusing the power struggle while laying the groundwork for a win-win solution.

For example:

> *"Honey, I can understand why you'd like to go to that fraternity party. It's exciting to be with older kids, and I don't blame you a bit to wanting to go. "*

LIMITS. The second part of the FLAC Method is to remind your teen of the limits of the situation and provide a good reason for those limits. It's much less provocative to say, "because the situation calls for this," rather than, "because I said so."

For example,

> *"But the fact is that you are sixteen years old and those kids are in college— some five or six years older than you. There's going to be drinking and maybe even drug use. Plus, some older guys see nothing wrong with pressuring younger girls into sex. This is not a situation that you should be in right now."*

ALTERNATIVES. If you leave it at that, you have softened the "no," but you haven't really helped your daughter solve her problem. The next step, looking for alternatives together, communicates that you really do care about her happiness and not just the rules. Plus, it teaches the valuable skill of creative thinking. In other words, you can't always solve a problem by attacking it head on, but if you open your mind to all possible solutions and avoid anger or self-pity, you can often find an acceptable alternative. Once people disengage from a struggle for power, you'd be surprised how often an acceptable alternative can be found.

For example:

> *"Let's put our heads together and see if we can find something else for you do that night that might be fun and safe."*

CONSEQUENCES. By the time you get to the C in FLAC, you might not need it: your teen might be able to stay on track without you setting a consequence for misbehavior. However, if you see that your teen needs an extra measure of motivation to stay within your limits, set a consequence that logically fits the situation. It does not need to be harsh—just enough to remind your teen that she is responsible for her actions. Even if you choose not to add a consequence at this point, be ready to add one later if your teen should violate your limits.

For example:

> *"Part of the privilege of having use of a car is being honest about where you're going and abiding by our decisions about where you can go. You've never given us a reason to take this privilege away from you, and I don't expect that this party will be the first time."*

Family Meeting: Problem Solving Using the FLAC Method

The FLAC Method is an effective process for solving family problems as well as individual ones. Whether you have regularly scheduled family meetings or you call a meeting only when you need to solve a problem or end a power struggle, FLAC can help. Before you use it for the first time, you'll want to explain the method to your family by going over the steps. Next, identify the problem you or another family member wants to solve. For example, in the *Active Parenting of Teens* video, the parents bring up the problem of their son Alex's falling grades. Then they proceed through the four steps:

Feelings: Each person shares thoughts and feelings about the problem, keeping the focus on the problem and not the person. The parents also show empathy and concern for their son and his feelings of frustration. They acknowledge that sometimes it's more fun to go out with friends than study.

Limits: Once Alex's parents have established a degree of empathy, they remind their son of the limits of the situation: that studying needs to be his number one priority because it will help him succeed in life.

Alternatives: Next, the family brainstorms alternatives and arrives at a decision to set a regular study time each school night until Alex gets his grades back on track. Although Alex isn't crazy about this idea, he accepts that it's the best solution to the problem. The goal of such problem solving is not to find a solution that everyone is in love with, but rather one that everybody can live with.

Consequences: The parents agree that there will not need to be a regular study time on weekends for now, but they will check back after the first grading period. If Alex's grades are still down, then the logical consequence will be that weekend study periods are added to the solution.

Besides discipline problems, you can also use the FLAC Method to make family decisions such as where to go out to eat, how to spend a fun day together, where to go for a family vacation, how to divide chores, curfews, use of the car, and any other decision in which affects your family. In these cases, keep in mind the following guidelines:

Every person has an equal voice. Although it may be difficult for parents to give up some of their authority, problem-solving discussions don't work well unless every person has an equal voice in the decisions made. Everyone in your family, including small children, needs to feel that he will be heard and can make a difference in what your family decides to do. Teens will not be very enthusiastic about family meetings, nor will they derive much benefit from them, if the meetings are merely forums for parents to hand down decisions that they have already made about the family.

In order to make decisions that are reasonable and fair to everyone, your family needs to hear everyone's opinions and feelings, even the negative ones.

Everyone may share what she thinks and feels about each issue. It is important that you promote an encouraging environment at your meetings, so that every person feels welcome to speak up and say what she thinks and feels about whatever question is on the table. In order to make decisions that are reasonable and fair to everyone, your family needs to hear everyone's opinions and feelings, even the negative ones.

Decisions are made by consensus. Reaching a consensus means that when there is disagreement, the parties involved discuss the matter until everyone agrees. It does not mean a vote is taken and the majority rules. If your family cannot reach consensus on a particular issue, choose one of two courses of action: either table the matter until the next meeting, when it will be discussed further, or (if it requires immediate action) exercise your duty as head of the household to make a decision and carry it out.

All decisions are in effect until the next meeting. Whatever decisions your family makes at a problem-solving meeting, uphold them at least until the next meeting, when they can be discussed again. Respond to complaints about these decisions by saying, "Bring it up again at the next meeting."

Some decisions are reserved for parents to make. Having family meetings does not imply that parents must always do whatever their children decide to do. Issues that affect the family's health and welfare are parental responsibilities, and the decision is sometimes theirs alone to make. But always allow and encourage discussion. For example, if Mom's employer tells her that she must move her family to a different city, she can't ask her children for approval. However, she can allow them to express their thoughts, concerns and feelings about the move, and to share in the planning.

Parenting and Anger

The management of anger has become recognized in recent years as vitally important to families and throughout society. Anger that turns to rage and then to violence creates headlines that range from school shootings and terrorist attacks to family violence. Even on smaller scales, children and adults who cannot control their temper create pain for themselves and those around them. Yet anger is also a natural part of life, so we are not quite sure what to make of this complicated emotion. Perhaps these pages will give you a new view of an old subject.

Many parents have difficulty controlling their anger, and as a result, the anger amplifies existing negative situations in the family and creates new problems. In an anger-filled family environment, teens' self-esteem and courage decline. Power struggles become more common, as does teens' desire for revenge. Anger is a sure-fire way to damage parent-teen relationships.

Teens are not always the victims, of course. Many teens are also prone to anger themselves. Those who respond to frustration with excessive anger often cause damage to themselves and others and can be painful to live with. Learning to manage anger effectively is crucial for everyone in the family.

The Anatomy of Anger

Anger is an emotional and physiological response to frustration. If we have an important need, want, or goal but find it blocked, one way our brains can react is to discharge powerful chemicals that prepare us mentally and physically to fight or run. We identify these intense chemical reactions as anger.

For example, a caveman walking through the woods comes upon a fallen tree that blocks his path. On the other side of the tree are some berries he wants to pick and eat. He strains to push the fallen tree aside, but he isn't strong enough, and he becomes frustrated at the thought of not reaching his goal. His frustration produces physiological changes in his body that enable him to lift the fallen tree savagely and hurl it aside.

Rudolph Dreikurs: People do not "lose" their tempers; they "use" their tempers.

Even in modern societies, anger can be useful. Rudolf Dreikurs once said that people do not "lose" their tempers; they "use" their tempers. What he meant was that people sometimes use anger to intimidate others into giving them what they want. Since anger is often accompanied by violence, this intimidation can sometimes be effective. But it carries a heavy price. Anger used to bully others damages relationships and is hurtful. Worse yet, it can lead to violent behavior and crime.

The Message of Anger

Our own angry feelings tell us that one of our goals is being blocked. Our brains clearly send us this message:

"Act! Don't just sit there; get up and do something!"

If we do something soon, we can often solve the problem before it gets worse, and before we "blow up." If we don't act but try to ignore the message, several things could happen:

1. The problem might go away by other means, but this is a risky and uncertain possibility.

2. Our anger may grow in intensity until it propels us into some action, which is likely to be desperate, unthinking, and potentially violent.

3. Our anger will seethe internally, expressing itself in unexpected ways: headaches, rashes, ulcers—even heart attacks.

How to Act on Anger

When a goal is blocked and our brains send us the message of anger, there are a number of useful ways to take positive action to solve the problem. We'll use the caveman's problem with the fallen tree to illustrate each method, and then we'll explain how this translates to using Active Parenting skills.

1. **Act to change the situation. Do something different.**

    Caveman: *Struggle until you remove the fallen tree. Invent a tree-remover.*

    Parent: *Use effective discipline skills such as "I" messages, logical consequences, and the FLAC method.*

2. **Reduce the importance of the goal. Put it in perspective.**
    ***Think* something different.**

    Caveman: *Although you may want the berries very much, be aware that you don't really need them for your survival.*

    Parent: *Let's say your teen still forgets to remove his dirty dishes from the den after you have asked and used an "I" message. Remind yourself that learning takes time, and a positive relationship with your teen is more important than dirty dishes.*

3. **Change your goals. Find an alternative. Again, think something different.**

    Caveman: *Decide that the berries are not the only solution to the hunger problem and look for an alternative—maybe an apple tree nearby.*

    Parent: *Give up your goal of having your teen play the piano and encourage an alternative activity of her choice.*

Helping Teens Use Their Anger

Because the executive center of the brain—the part that controls emotions—is the last part to develop, teens' expression of anger and frustration may be more like the caveman rather than a mature adult. Tantrums and hitting are fairly common with young children, but even into adolescence some kids have trouble expressing anger with restraint. In these days of "zero tolerance" for aggressive behavior, it's essential that we teach teens that violence is not an OK way to solve problems. There are several ways parents can help:

Give them a good model. The way you handle your own problems and frustrations will provide a model for your teens. Ask yourself:

- Do you fly into a rage, hurling insults and humiliating remarks?

- Do you strike out at others?

- Do you sink into a depression (which is sometimes an adult temper tantrum or "silent storm")?

Guide them with words to find more effective forms of expression. For example:

"You have the right to feel the way you do, but in our family, we don't scream and blame; we look for solutions."

"I can see that you're angry. But you need to talk to me about it instead of hitting."

"When you get angry at me, please tell me without calling me names. I don't call you names. I don't expect you to call me names."

Remove yourself from a power struggle. When teens are inappropriate in their anger, it's OK for you to acknowledge the anger, but at the same time "take your sails out of their wind." Don't try to win and don't give in; withdraw instead. This action says, "I am not intimidated by your

show of temper and will not give in, but I won't punish or humiliate you either." The result is that teens who get neither a fight nor their own way after throwing tantrums will usually find more acceptable ways to influence people. If you need a quiet place to withdraw from the power struggle, try the bathroom. It's the one place where a little privacy is usually expected.

Teach self-soothing techniques. Some teens are born with a more spirited temperament, and are more prone to losing control of their emotions. You can help these teens learn to manage their feelings with self-soothing techniques such as deep breathing, time-out, listening to calming music (not stimulating music), taking a warm bath, meditation, and other methods. Find a time when you are both calm to discuss the problem and decide which methods you will try together.

Use the FLAC Method to solve problems. In cases where a teen's anger interferes with the rights of others, the FLAC method can defuse the situation. You can acknowledge the feeling, remind him of the limits, work together to find an alternative, and follow through with logical consequences.

Be clear that violence is never an acceptable way to getting what you want. Even intimidation or threats of violence are to be treated firmly. Take the time to discuss why this is a family value, and why it's the law.

Family Enrichment Activity: Positive "I" Messages

We learned earlier in this chapter that "I" messages offer parents an effective way to confront their teens about repeated misbehavior. They are clear, firm, calm communications that are often easy for teens to hear without becoming defensive. These same qualities of "I" messages also make them useful as encouraging statements when teens are behaving well, particularly when, in response to discipline, your teen has made an effort to correct her behavior. Positive "I" messages, as we call them, can help motivate a teen to continue improving her behavior.

For example, let's say Alex keeps his agreement with his parents and begins some serious studying. His parents can use a positive "I" message like this:

1. State what you like.

   "I like how you're keeping your agreement and really using your study time."

2. Say how you feel.

   "I feel good knowing that you're making an effort to improve your grades."

3. Tell them why.

   "... because I want you to have the best opportunities in life you can have."

4. Offer to do something that will support his effort.

   "How about if I bring you a snack in a few minutes to keep those brain cells fed?"

You may have noticed that this fourth step is a new concept. When you learned how to use "I" messages as a method of discipline, the fourth step was to tell your teen what behavior change you want. Now that you have that change, you can encourage your teen's effort by offering him something that will promote his continued success. Just make sure that this fourth step doesn't become a reward. It will help to keep the offer logically connected to your teen's positive behavior, as Alex's parents did in the previous example. You might even think of this as a "positive logical consequence."

Don't worry if you don't use every step of the positive "I" message every time. The first step (*State what you like.*) is encouraging by itself. And feel free to use your own words so that the message feels natural to you.

chapter **3**

Home Activities

1. Practice using polite requests, "I" messages, and firm reminders, and fill out the guide sheets on pages 106-107.

2. Practice using a logical consequence and complete the guide sheet on page 109.

3. For your family meeting, use the FLAC Method to work through a problem that your family is having.

4 For your family enrichment activity, catch your teen improving his behavior this week and give a positive "I" message to encourage him to keep up the good work.

Basic Discipline Practice

Use the questions on these pages to get some practice with the three methods of basic discipline that you learned in this chapter: Polite Requests, "I" Messages, and Firm Reminders.

1. Pretend that your teen has just talked to you disrespectfully. Write an example of a **polite request** that you could use to handle the problem:

   _____

   _____

2. Let's assume that your teen continues to speak disrespectfully to you. Construct an **"I" message** that you could give her:

   I have a problem with _____

   I feel _____

   because _____

   I would like (or *Will you please*) _____

3. Now let's assume that the "I" message was not effective. Construct a firm reminder for your teen:

   _____

   _____

Home Example

4. Write down a problem that you own from your own family: _____

   _____

   _____

Continued on the next page...

5. Now write an "I" message that you can use at home this week to solve the problem:

I have a problem with _____

I feel _____

because _____

I would like (or *Will you please*) _____

Evaluation

6. How did your teen respond to your "I" message? _____

_____

_____

7. What did you like about the way you delivered the "I" message?_____

_____

_____

8. How would you do it differently next time? _____

_____

_____

Logical Consequences Video Practice

Scene	Guideline Violated	Possible Logical Consequences
1. Jada: messy living room		
2. Julie: leaving the car without gas		
3. Matt: cleaning up his web page		
4. Derrick: late for dinner		

This guide sheet refers to the Active Parenting of Teens *discussion program. If you are using this Parent's Guide independently and are interested in participating in a discussion group, check out our web site for information:*
www.ActiveParenting.com/ParentingTeens

Using Logical Consequences

Think of a problem you'd like to solve using a logical consequence. (You may want to choose the same problem for which you constructed an "I" message on pages 106-107 if that "I" message was not effective.)

Write in the space below one way that you might present the choices and consequences to your teen during the discussion of the problem. _____

_____

Meet with your teen to discuss the problem, and use this logical consequence or one that you develop together.

Evaluation

What was your teen's response to the discussion? _____

_____

What was his response to the logical consequence? (Did he test you to see if you would follow through?)

_____

_____

If the consequence isn't working, do you think you need to stick with it longer or change the consequence to something else?_____

_____

If the consequence isn't working, have you violated any of the guidelines for setting up logical consequences? _____

_____

What do you like about the way you handled the use of logical consequences? _____

_____

What will you do differently next time? _____

_____

Building Courage, Redirecting Misbehavior

Fifteen-year-old Matt had been having a very bad week. First, a "D" on his biology test. *Guess I should have studied*, he thought to himself gloomily. To make matters worse, his younger sister, Abby, had come home with an "A" on her social studies test. The way his parents were crowing over her was enough to make him sick. He retreated to his room to get away from them, and turned up his music. Now he was staring moodily at the mirror. *Yep, breaking out all over. What a loser. Well, at least I have a good body*, he told himself as he flexed a muscle. *Isn't that what girls are supposed to care about?* Then his heart sank as he remembered the teasing from his best friend, Steve. "If you get out of tenth grade still a virgin, I'm gonna kick your butt." Steve had had sex for the first time in eighth grade. He had a lot of confidence around girls. *Which of course I don't*, thought Matt. He thought about the upcoming party on Saturday night. *Maybe that's when it can happen with Julie.* After all, this was their third date. A lot of guys Matt knew—Steve among them—only needed a couple of hours with a girl to score. *Maybe if I can get her to down a couple of drinks....*

Courage: One from the Heart

The teen years are rife with ups and downs, angst, and discouragement. Very few get through it unscathed, and those who do are likely to find their share of hardship later in life. It can be tough keeping spirits up when it seems like the world is conspiring to bring them down, and sometimes it's tempting to grasp at low hanging values in a misguided effort to keep going. It takes courage to hold out for the "higher" values: to hang in there and keep working when self-doubt grips the heart and twists. In the story you've just read, Matt lacks that courage. In other words, he has become *dis*-couraged. Like most teens, he is struggling to balance the pressures of school, social life, and family with the rapid changes he is experiencing in his own intellectual, physical, and emotional development. His failures have hit him particularly hard. He beats himself up with his own negative perceptions. Matt has lost heart.

We learned earlier that the French word *coeur*, meaning "heart," is the base of the English word *courage*. Just as the heart has long been considered the center of human emotions, courage might be thought of as the core of a person's character.

Courage is intimately linked to fear. Everyone experiences this two-sided coin at some point in life, especially during times of risk. *Do I go ahead or turn back? What if I fail? What if they reject me? Do I dare to take the chance?* It is our courage that keeps us going when the easier path is to quit or give in to an unwise temptation. Because striving for most positive goals in life requires some risk, courage is essential. For a teen to become responsible, he has to risk the consequences of his choices. To cooperate, he has to risk that others may take advantage of him. Honesty, hard work, even love—these all require some risk.

If a teen doesn't know the consequences of a risk he decides to take, then the act isn't courageous; it's foolish and reckless.

In Chapter 2, we defined **courage** as: **the confidence to take a known risk for a known purpose**. This definition is based on how well one understands the risk in question. If a teen doesn't know the consequences of a risk he decides to take, then the act isn't courageous; it's foolish and reckless. The same is true for someone who takes a risk without knowing the potential drawbacks and benefits of doing so. For example, the teen who takes drugs for the thrill of it, thinking nothing bad will happen to her, is not being courageous. She doesn't know the real risks. Contrast this with the teen who makes an "F" on a test but decides to study for hours to do better on the next one. He is showing a lot of courage, a lot of character.

Self-Esteem: One from the Mind

Where does this teen's courage come from? It comes from a belief in himself: the belief that regardless of any particular outcome, he is a lovable, capable person who has a good chance to succeed. And when he doesn't succeed, he looks inward for a belief that he is much more than just his achievements—that there is something worthwhile and special about him just because he is himself. This belief—his high

Courage & Fear

Courage first met fear
When I was still a child;
Courage gazed with cool, clear eyes;
Fear was something wild.

Courage urged, "Let's go ahead."
Fear said, "Let's turn back."
Courage spoke of what we had;
Fear of what we lacked.

Courage took me by the hand
And warmed my frozen bones;
Yet Fear the while tugged at my legs
And whispered, "We're alone."

Many have been the obstacles
Since first I had to choose,
And sometimes when Courage led me on
I've come up with a bruise.

And many have been the challenges
Since Fear and Courage met,
And yet those times I've followed Fear,
Too often—tagged along Regret.

by Michael H. Popkin

self-esteem—helps motivate him to continue to work hard for good grades even after he has received a low one. It gives him the confidence to say "no" to his friends when they invite him to goof off instead of study, or even when they pressure him to use drugs or engage in other destructive behavior.

When self-esteem is high—when we think we have a reasonable chance to succeed, and we know that all is not lost if we don't—we have the confidence to tackle life's challenges. We have courage.

High Self-esteem ➡ *Courage*

Unfortunately, the opposite is also true. When we think badly of ourselves—that we are unlovable or not capable—our self-esteem drops. This low self-esteem produces discouragement and fear.

Low Self-esteem ➡ *Discouragement*

Teens with high self-esteem have the courage to take positive risks, while teens with low self-esteem either don't bother taking risks at all, or they take unwise risks in a reckless effort to feel better for a little while. For example:

TEENS WITH HIGH SELF-ESTEEM...	TEENS WITH LOW SELF-ESTEEM...
■ tackle hard problems at school, even if it increases his chances of making mistakes.	■ develop an "I don't care" attitude towards school and stop working or even drop out.
■ do what she knows is right even if she loses her friends in the process.	■ change her values to conform to those of her peers
■ cooperate with parents even when he doesn't always get his way.	■ resent authority and rebel, either openly or passively, through intentional failure and other means
■ find positive ways (e.g. sports) to achieve independence and challenge.	■ resort to easier, negative behavior (e.g. drugs, sexuality, and violence) to achieve independence and challenge.

The Think-Feel-Do Cycle

Before we can effectively influence teens, we first need some understanding of what motivates them. Let's consider how four separate aspects of a teen's motivation are related: events (something that happens in the teen's life); thoughts (including his beliefs, attitudes and values); feelings; and behavior. We call this the "Think-Feel-Do Cycle".

The Think-Feel-Do Cycle

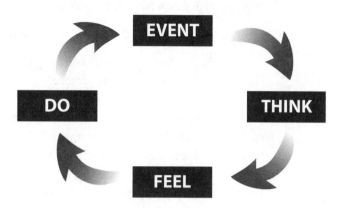

This is how the cycle works: When something happens to a teen (an event), he thinks about it, both consciously and unconsciously. All of his attitudes, needs, and values about such situations and about himself come into play. This thinking then produces a feeling. Many people mistakenly believe that feelings just happen, but they are really products of our thoughts and values. Change the thinking and you change the feelings, too. Together, the thinking and feeling produce an action (behavior). As the event changes or remains the same, the teen will have new thoughts, feelings, and behavior as the system goes around and around.

Here's an example. Shelly is a quiet teen who one day saw another girl sitting alone in the cafeteria (The Event). She thought to herself that this looked like a good opportunity to try and make a friend (Think) and mustered the courage (Feel) to approach the other girl and ask if she could join her (Do). The other girl responded positively (Event) and Shelly sat down with her. Before long they were talking together about all kinds of things, and when lunch was over, Shelly had a good feeling inside. That afternoon, she found herself more talkative than usual in class, and she carried her good feeling throughout the day. The next day at lunch she sought out her new friend, and again they shared a pleasant meal, this time making plans to see a movie together over the weekend. Shelly's courage was rewarded with a new friend, and she has moved into a success cycle where positive thoughts trigger positive feelings and behavior and lead to positive events and success.

Now let's see how the Think-Feel-Do Cycle reveals Matt's thought process from this chapter's opening story. Let's start with his biology test. His thinking about this event may have included some of the following:

Values: *"Doing well in school is important."*

Beliefs: *"I blew it. I knew I wasn't very smart. Abby is the smart one in the family. I'm pretty pathetic."*

These negative thoughts lowered his self-esteem and triggered negative feelings, such as anger, sadness, and discouragement. These feelings led to more negative behavior on Matt's part, as we will soon see.

Of course, there is always more than one event going on at a time in a teen's life. Matt is being influenced by lots of events, such as his other school subjects, his family, his friends, and his social life. When more than one event goes sour at the same time, the resulting stress is multiplied. This is what happens to Matt as he thinks and feels about his acne, how he compares to his sister, and his lack of sexual experience.

Tolerating setbacks and disappointments requires courage. When a teen's courage is low, he often looks for a quick way to reduce his pain. If he has an interest or hobby, such as sports or music, he can focus on this as a positive way to help him feel better about himself. Or he could choose another positive outlet such as talking to someone who cares about him. Unfortunately, teens sometimes turn to negative behavior to get some temporary relief. Let's see how this plays out in Matt's case...

When Matt finally got out of bed Sunday morning, his head hurt and he had a queasy feeling in his stomach. He cringed as the events of the night before began to come back to him. How could he have been so stupid? Everything had been going great with Julie. Then he had started drinking. *Well, so what*, he thought as he shuffled to the mirror to examine his bleary eyes. *It was a party, wasn't it?* Matt sat back down on the edge of the bed and tried to remember what had happened next. *Oh yeah*. He groaned. Steve had told him about the empty bedroom upstairs and had handed him a condom. *Why didn't I just laugh and walk away?*

He remembered escorting Julie to the bedroom. They were laughing, and Julie seemed to be having fun. He made her a drink with the vodka he'd smuggled out of his house in a water bottle—So far, so good.—But then he'd pulled out the condom and it was all downhill from there. Julie had said something like, "You've got to be kidding!" That wasn't part of the plan. He was a little fuzzy about what had happened next except that vodka had spilled all over the bed and suddenly Julie was really mad— pushing him away and getting up to leave, and then he was alone. As these details came back to him, Matt put his head in his hands. *Just let me curl up and die*, he thought.

The Failure Cycle

When a teen reacts to events in his life with low self-esteem and a poorly developed system of values, the discouragement and negative behavior that follow usually produce more negative events. In Matt's case, these events might include getting dumped by Julie, increasing alcohol abuse, and more failed tests in school. In addition, teen misbehavior often provokes harsh criticism and punishment from autocratic adults, which triggers more faulty thinking and lower self-esteem, more discouragement, and more negative behavior and failure.

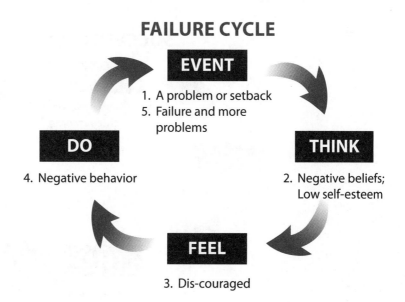

FAILURE CYCLE

EVENT
1. A problem or setback
5. Failure and more problems

THINK
2. Negative beliefs; Low self-esteem

FEEL
3. Dis-couraged

DO
4. Negative behavior

The Success Cycle

A teen with higher self-esteem than Matt's and more positive beliefs about himself might have responded much differently to the failed biology test. He may have thought, *Face it. I blew it. I'll have to study big time for the next one to make up for this.* Such thinking may have produced some feelings of remorse for having done poorly on the test, but it would not cause discouragement. In fact, a teen with high self-esteem and a well-developed set of values can take failure and turn it into a positive experience, one in which he learns from his mistakes. This positive behavior usually produces additional successful events, including positive feedback from adults. These successes strengthen self-esteem and courage, motivating the teen to produce more effort and positive behavior and thus more success. This "success cycle" can be summed up by the popular expression "nothing succeeds like success".

A teen with high self-esteem and a well-developed set of values can take failure and turn it into a positive experience, one in which he learns from his mistakes.

Julie is a good example of a teen in a success cycle. Her high self-esteem and mature attitude about sexuality gave her the courage to resist Matt's advances. She stood up for herself and took positive action to solve the problem by leaving. She will feel good when she thinks later about how she handled herself. Her self-esteem will strengthen, and she'll feel encouraged to stand up for herself the next time she is threatened.

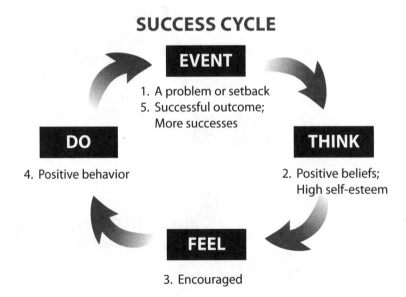

SUCCESS CYCLE

EVENT
1. A problem or setback
5. Successful outcome;
   More successes

THINK
2. Positive beliefs;
   High self-esteem

FEEL
3. Encouraged

DO
4. Positive behavior

When your teen is discouraged, it's important that you help her avoid or break out of a failure cycle. When she's encouraged, your role is to help her continue to thrive in a success cycle. To do both requires a skillful blend of discipline and encouragement. We covered discipline in detail in the last chapter. Now, let's look more closely at developing encouragement skills.

Four Ways We Sometimes Discourage

There are many ways to encourage your teen, and they all begin with the same first step: recognize and avoid ways that you inadvertently *dis*courage them.

> en*courage* = *"to give courage"*
> dis*courage* = *"to remove courage"*

It may not always seem like it, but parents are very important people in teens' lives. What they say and do can have an enormous effect on their teens.

It may not always seem like it, but parents are very important people in teens' lives. What they say and do can have an enormous effect on their teens. Try putting yourself in a teen's shoes as you read about four of the most common ways parents discourage their teens. Then look for ways to catch yourself before you make these mistakes with your own teen.

1. Focusing on mistakes and weaknesses

If someone important to you spends more time pointing out your faults than your strengths, you may come to believe there is much more wrong with you than right. If that person yells or sounds disgusted with you, calls you names and attacks your character, you may begin to believe you are as bad as he says. Improvement seems impossible. This is how a teen feels when his parent constantly points out his mistakes.

Examples:

> *"You are so lazy! I don't know why I even bother!"*

> *"If you want to get anywhere in life, you're going to have to stop being so shy."*

> *"I just can't see any reason for this C in geometry." (said while ignoring the As and Bs in other subjects)*

2. Expecting the worst or too little

If you don't believe in your teen's abilities, your teen probably won't believe in them either. Parents don't always express these low expectations overtly, but teens get the message loud and clear, regardless.

Examples:

"I knew you'd start cutting school like those losers you hang out with. Next, you'll be dropping out."

"You'd better stay out of trouble while I'm gone."

"Girls have a harder time in math than boys, so a C is pretty good."

3. Expecting too much (perfectionism)

On the other hand, if you expect more from your teen than she is able to give, she may gradually stop trying or suffer severely from low self-esteem. No matter what she accomplishes, she will never satisfy you—or so it seems to her. Parents often excuse their too-high expectations by saying that they merely want the best for their children. But their desire for the best often does more harm than good. Teens may give up trying to please their parents and do an about-face, instead excelling in negative pursuits like drug abuse or promiscuous sex. For teens who become perfectionists in a futile attempt to please their parents and themselves, life becomes one big worry. Hidden behind the façade of "having it all together" is often a very fragile self-image and low self-esteem.

Examples:

"Don't get conceited; you still have a lot of room for improvement."

"I'll bet if you lost five pounds, you'd look great in that dress."

"You're already great in track. Why aren't you on the varsity soccer team?"

4.   Overprotecting and pampering

If you're constantly telling your teen how dangerous the world is and preventing him from taking even reasonable risks, he may begin to believe that he can't handle things for himself. If you constantly step in and protect her from the consequences of her poor choices, you rob her of the opportunity to learn from experience. Your teen may become extremely dependent on you and expect you to take over all his problems. Alternately, he may rebel and take reckless risks just to show that you can't run his life.

Some parents act more like personal servants than parents, providing wake-up service, maid service, taxi service without notice, short-order cooking, and any other buffers needed to protect their teen from the realities of life. Not surprisingly, teens brought up this way form unrealistic ideas about how the world works. As these teens reach adulthood, they often lack motivation to work hard or do things for themselves. They expect things to be easy. When they aren't, they'll become frustrated and angry.

Examples:

> *"If you're not ready to take that science test, why don't you let me write you a sick note so you can study some more?"*

> *"Well, I really need to get this report done, but if it means that much to you, I'll drive you to the mall."*

> *"I'm going to sit right here and help you with your homework like I always do."*

Turning Discouragement into Encouragement

Fortunately, each of the four ways we often discourage teens can be turned around and become ways to encourage them:

Turn Discouragers	...into Encouragers
Focus on mistakes and weaknesses	Build on strengths
Expect the worst or too little	Show confidence
Expect too much (perfectionism)	Value the teen as-is
Overprotect and pamper	Stimulate independence

These methods of encouragement are effective not only with teens, but also with co-workers, spouses, and other adults. After all, who doesn't need some self-esteem and courage reinforcement sometimes? Let's look at the four methods more closely.

1. Build on Strengths

If you want a teen to do better in general, find something you like about her. When you focus on her strengths rather than her weaknesses, she feels encouraged to build more strengths. For example:

"I really like your enthusiasm—the way you jump in with both feet."

"You have a great sense of humor."

"I have to tell you, even though we argue a lot, I really admire how you stand up for yourself. That will be valuable throughout your life."

Focusing on your teen's strengths is a great way to build his self-esteem, courage and positive behavior in general. But it can also help improve a specific skill, value, or character trait. Whether you are helping a teen do better with a school subject or to be more respectful, keep in mind the following four steps of what I've named "The BANK Method."

The BANK Method of Encouragement

Break it down into Baby steps.

Acknowledge strengths.

Nudge to take the next step.

Keep encouraging!

To help you remember how effectively encourage your teen by building on her strengths, keep in mind the four letters of B-A-N-K. Just as a bank is a place where resources are invested for growth, you can use the BANK method to help your teen build her personal assets and grow into a successful human being. Let's look at the four letters one by one:

Remember, you didn't learn to walk all at once. You learned step by step. This learning process is the same for most tasks.

B for Break it down into Baby steps. The key to building on strengths is to break the goal down into small steps that are easily accomplished. Success at each step becomes the encouragement that motivates the teen to keep working towards the ultimate goal. Remember, you didn't learn to walk all at once. You learned step by step. This learning process is the same for most tasks. Whether it is helping a child learn to complete his homework, or teaching him to be honest, we can systematically build on strengths to help our teens develop skills, values, and character. For example:

> *"I know school can be difficult, but if we break each assignment down into small steps, you can do it."*

> *"If we want to teach Danielle to be honest, I think we need to encourage her every time she tells the truth when she could have lied or deceived us."*

A for Acknowledge what your teen does well. Once you have identified a goal for him (for example, developing good study habits or being honest), get an idea where he is on the path towards reaching that goal. It is unlikely that he can't read a single word or answers every question with a lie—so he will be somewhere in between. Now you have a place to start. Acknowledge what he can already do well in order to build confidence and motivation to take the next step. For example:

> *"I'm not thrilled that you borrowed the car without asking, but I do appreciate your owning up to it when I asked. I appreciate your honesty."*

It is much more effective to "catch 'em doing good" than the traditional approach of catching them doing bad. In addition to acknowledging their progress, it also helps to acknowledge other areas where the teen is already experiencing some success. This helps build the self-esteem that translates into risk taking and other successes.

> *"This is terrific! You've completed two assignments. This is the way to get ahead at school. I can really see that you've worked hard at this, but then I know you can work hard… I've seen you on the basketball court."*

N for Nudge your teen to take the next step. Teens get a sense of self-esteem from learning, whether it's a sport, a school subject, or a character trait. As we have seen, learning requires many steps and gradual improvement. It also requires risk, because with each new step, there is the potential for failure. Even with teens who have high self-esteem, there are times when fear of failure makes it difficult for them to take the next step. And there are times for all of us when the frustration of not progressing the way we'd like undermines our courage to persevere and tempts us to give up. This is when an encouraging nudge from a parent, teacher, other adult, or peer can help give the teen enough courage to take the next baby step. For example:

> *"Learning algebra can be frustrating, and I guess you feel like giving up. But if you'll just stick with it, I know you'll get it. Look how far you've come already! "*

> *"I know it hasn't been easy, but you've really improved in being honest with us. And we're feeling like we can trust you more. So, if you still want to spend the night at Carrie's house, it's okay with us."*

> *"You can do it. Go ahead."*

> *"Keep trying. You'll get it."*

> *"Sometimes a rest can help. Let's try again tomorrow."*

K for Keep encouraging improvement and effort. Arthur Blank, co-founder of The Home Depot and owner of the Atlanta Falcons pro football team, once said that although he is a highly competitive person, he never sees the finish line. In other words, life is a process in which success is measured by growth and improvement rather than by the end result. The mistake most people make in the encouragement process is to wait until the teen attains a desired goal before offering encouragement. I even heard from one misguided father who actually said that he was waiting for his son to graduate before complimenting him on his schoolwork! Since a key to encouragement is to break the process down into baby steps, it is important to offer encouragement with each step along the route. Any improvement, no matter how small, is a step in the right direction and should be noticed and acknowledged. Success is a great motivator, so help your teen to experience numerous successes along the way. This builds self-esteem and keeps him moving towards the goal. If he falls back a step (and that's to be expected), he needs encouragement to keep at it and not give up. In fact, his effort alone, even when he's not making progress, should always be encouraged. For example:

Any improvement, no matter how small, is a step in the right direction and should be noticed and acknowledged. Success is a great motivator.

> *"Great! You are really getting good at writing down all of your assignments. One more day and you'll have a whole week."*

> *"I can really see the effort that went into this."*

> *"Hey, this room is really looking good. You've gotten all your books picked up, and the bed's made. If you like, I have some time and could help you figure out a system for organizing your closet."*

> *"I really like the way you stick with it."*

2. Show Confidence

Teens develop self-esteem and courage by developing skills and learning how to handle problems. But to do this, they need self-esteem and courage. You can cut into this "chicken and egg" situation by giving your teen responsibility, asking her opinion or advice, and avoiding unnecessary rescues.

Give Responsibility. Giving your teen responsibility is a nonverbal way of showing confidence. It says, "I know you can do this." Of course, be careful to give responsibilities that are in line with the teen's age and level of ability, or you are setting him up for failure. For example:

> *"It would be a big help if you would take over cooking dinner one night a week."*

"Would you be willing to take responsibility for the garage sale? I'll help if you need it, but I've got so much to do this week, and I know you'd do a good job."

"I'll agree to your going to the party if you'll agree that if there's any alcohol or other drugs there, you will call us to pick you up immediately."

Ask your teen's opinion or advice. The teen years are filled with rapid intellectual growth. You can help encourage this development, as well as the self-esteem and courage that can go with it, by asking your teen's opinion or advice. You can even ask her to teach you something.

Examples:

"I'm having trouble sending messages on this new phone. Would you show me how to do it?"

"Something came up at work today, and I wanted to know what you thought about it."

"Now that you'll be dating soon, we'd like your help in setting some guidelines so that we can all feel comfortable with the situation."

A word of caution: Be careful to avoid turning your teen into a confidante or best friend. Sharing intimate personal problems can sometimes feel good, especially for a single parent, but it can be an unfair burden on your teen. Look for a close friend or a counselor for this type of adult sharing.

Sometimes teens can solve problems on their own. You can offer support and encouragement without robbing your teen of the self-esteem that comes from struggle and success.

Avoid unnecessary rescues. Some problems require parental involvement, but sometimes teens can solve problems on their own. When you refuse to step in and take over when your teen becomes frustrated or discouraged, you're showing confidence in her abilities. You can offer support and encouragement without robbing her of the self-esteem that comes from struggle and success.

Examples:

"Keep trying. You can do it!"

"I know this is hard for you. Can you think of anything that would help you work it out?"

3. Value Your Teen As-Is

Your teen's self-esteem does not come from his achievements alone. His courage and self-respect also relies upon feeling accepted by significant people in his life. In fact, this is often what everyone wants most: to be accepted for who they really are, not just for what they've accomplished.

Your teen needs to know that win or lose, pass or fail, in trouble or out of trouble, you are still his parent, and *you are glad of it.* Everyone needs this unconditional love from someone. This is why parenting programs that advocate kicking a rebellious teen out of the house are off the mark. No parent should ever communicate to a teen that she is no longer part of the family. Parents should say just the opposite: "No matter what it takes—counseling, hospitalization, a therapy program—we're going to find a way for you to be a part of this family. We love you, and we're going to get you the help you need."

*Your teen needs to know that win or lose, pass or fail, in trouble or out of trouble, you are still his parent, and you are **glad** of it.*

Fortunately, most families don't ever have to deal with such an extreme situation, but all of us need to look at the subtle messages we give our teens and make sure that we focus on ways to value them as they are. Here are some ideas.

Separate the deed from the doer. Parents can help teens value themselves by separating who they are from what they do. When your teen misbehaves, focus your attention on the behavior, not the teen:

Focus on the deed:

> *"I don't like you talking to me that way. It's rude."*

> *"You failed the test because you didn't study enough, not because you're dumb."*

Not the doer:

> *"You are so rude."*

> *"You didn't fail because you're dumb. You failed because you're lazy."*

Even when encouraging your teen's positive behavior, focus on the behavior rather than the teen. Why? Because a teen's subconscious sounds something like this: "If I'm good when I do good, then I must be bad when I do bad." Once a teen concludes he is somehow bad, he gives up. You want your teen to learn that he is ultimately a good person, but that he sometimes chooses bad behavior. His choices are correctable.

You want your teen to learn that he is ultimately a good person, but that he sometimes chooses bad behavior. His choices are correctable.

Focus on the deed:

> *"That was really considerate of you to take your brother with you."*

> *"I really appreciate the way you help out around here."*

Not the doer:

> *"You are such a considerate person."*

> *"You are such a helpful young man."*

You can also help your teen learn to separate actions from self-worth by gently correcting him when he gets down on himself. For example:

> *"Missing two foul shots doesn't make you a loser. It can happen to even the best players."*

> *"You're not stupid. You made a mistake. I think you've learned something and will make a different choice next time."*

Appreciate your teen's uniqueness. Although we live in a society of equals, that doesn't mean we're all the same. It's important for your teen to know that she is one-of-a-kind, with her own unique dreams and talents. You can appreciate your teen's uniqueness by noticing these things. Most of all, you can say and do things that show your teen that you love her for being herself, and that you need no other reason.

Examples:

> *"This room really is 'you'! I could never have decorated it for you."*
>
> *"What do you dream about doing someday?"*
>
> *"You are the only you in the whole world. I'm so glad that you're my daughter!"*
>
> *"I love you."*

4. Stimulate Independence

Teens work hard to break away from their parents and become independent adults. Sometimes it's a hard truth for parents to accept. But keeping your teen overly dependent upon you is destined to backfire. As psychologist Hiam Ginott once wrote, "Dependence breeds hostility." So unless you are looking forward to someday having a hostile thirty-year-old son or daughter living with you, give your teen some independence and freedom. This will also reduce how much the two of you fight. And the more your teen succeeds at becoming independent, the higher his self-esteem and courage will rise.

Examples:

> *"I think going to camp for four weeks is a great idea. Let's talk about how you can help pay for it."*
>
> *"I'm okay with you taking a part-time job as long as it's no more than twenty hours a week and doesn't affect your schoolwork."*
>
> *"Consider this fair warning: From now on, when you want me to drive you somewhere, you need to let me know in advance and not expect me to drop what I'm doing to take you."*
>
> *"Running this house is the responsibility of all of us. I'd like us to have a family meeting to discuss which chores each of us will be doing."*

Allow your teen to take reasonable risks. Remember that courage is about having the confidence to take reasonable risks. Talk with other adults, including parents and educators, to get a feel for what others think are reasonable limits and freedoms for

The key is to allow your teen more and more independence while staying aware of how she handles each new step

teens of different ages in your community. Then talk with your teen about guidelines and expectations. The key is to allow your teen more and more independence while staying aware of how she handles each new step. If she does not handle the independence well, you can return to tighter limits next time. If she handles the independence responsibly, she has earned the right to more independence.

Examples:

> *"You may go to the concert as long as you follow the guidelines we've discussed."*
>
> *"The choice to play football is yours, but I'd like to talk with you about other sports that have less risk for a major injury."*
>
> *"Going to camp is a great way to develop your independence. So is getting a part-time job to help pay for it."*

The truth is that life in a democratic society is neither independent nor dependent; it is interdependent. One of the things this means for teens is that along with their emerging independence comes a desire to belong to new groups of friends. The ability to work with others becomes important around this time too. You can help encourage your teen to understand the give and take necessary for being a friend and how to work with others cooperatively.

Examples:

> *"You're an important part of this family, and we'd like your input at family meetings."*
>
> *"Would you like to help me change the oil in the car?"*
>
> *"Would you like me to help the two of you work out a fair plan for sharing the telephone?"*

Remember, every new skill requires practice to get it right. The guide sheets at the end of this chapter will help you practice using your new encouragement skills.

Self-Esteem, Courage, and Body Image

A growing body of evidence suggests that many girls experience a loss of self-esteem and courage when they hit adolescence. Girls who at age ten were active, confident, and enthusiastic about learning may change drastically in the early teen years, becoming less curious, less concerned about their long-term goals, and more worried about how they look and what others think about them.

Consider the female image presented in our media. Everywhere girls look—on billboards, in magazines, on TV—they see women whose primary function is to be beautiful and sexy. In print advertising, pictures of women are often altered to create unrealistic perfection: inches are shaved off the hips; skin tone is smoothed out; legs are lengthened. Supermodels often lead extreme lifestyles to support their body image, including drug use, surgery, and unhealthy dieting. At an age when girls are naturally putting on fat and are going through other hormonal changes, they are bombarded with images of women too thin to menstruate. Most adults realize that these are not realistic images of women, but many teen girls don't know that. There's little wonder that so many become bulimic or anorexic in an attempt to stay thin.

Teenage boys are not exempt from the unrealistic expectations that the media reinforces. Advertising is full of idealized images of men with sculpted bodies that are often only attainable through surgery or steroid use. We're seeing more and more incidents of eating disorders among boys and young men.

Breaking from Gender Stereotypes

What can you do to help counteract some of the negative messages society heaps on girls and boys about what it means to be women and men? Here are some ideas:

- Value your teenage girl's skills, especially academic abilities.

- Encourage her to be assertive about what she wants and needs, not just to support others.

- Encourage her to play one or more sports.

- Help her set long-term goals about what will make her happy, which may not include marriage and a family.

- Discuss with her what she needs to do to reach these goals.

- Expect as much from your daughter as your son.

- Teach your son to respect girls as equals, and not as sexual objects.

- Help your son and/or your daughter see how the media overemphasizes appearance and promotes unrealistic thinness.

- Encourage your son to participate in the arts and to express himself through drawing, writing, and similar pursuits.

- Teach teens of both sexes to notice and name their feelings, and treat these feelings as important information for understanding themselves and others.

- Provide your son with information about career options that are traditionally female, such as nursing, parenting, social work, and elementary education.

- Provide your daughter with information about career options that are traditionally male, such as science, information technology, finance, professional cooking, piloting, and business management.

- Help your son be comfortable with his body image and physical development.

- Help your son understand that having sex early and often is not a sign of manhood.

Understanding Teen Behavior: Purpose, Not Cause

We've established that teen behavior is influenced by outside events, including the style with which a teen is parented and how encouraging or discouraging the parents are. But we have also learned that these events do not directly *cause* the teen's behavior. Human beings have free will: we choose how to behave based on our genetic make-up, experience, values, and goals for the future. So, to understand why teen behaves the way he does, ask yourself,

> ***"What is the <u>purpose</u> or <u>goal</u> of his behavior?"***

> ***"What payoff is his behavior aimed at getting?"***

A person's goals influence his behavior, but since this occurs at an unconscious level, it is often difficult to know what motivates someone. For example, fourteen-year-old Jason wants to get a tattoo, but his parents are furious and absolutely forbid it. Jason does it anyway. Why has Jason refused to comply with his parents' orders? What is his purpose, or goal? To help us answer these questions, let's look at five basic goals that motivate much of teen behavior.

The Five Goals of Teen Behavior

In Chapter 1 you learned that the purpose of parenting is to protect and prepare your teens to survive and to thrive in the kind of society in which they will live. Building on the foundation laid by Alfred Adler and Rudolf Dreikurs, Active Parenting recognizes five goals that humans consider essential to surviving and thriving. These same five goals govern much of your teen's behavior:

- Belonging

- Power

- Protection

- Withdrawal

- Challenge

Let's look at each of these goals more closely, particularly as they appear during the teen years.

Belonging

The basic need of every human being is to belong. A baby could not survive without others to depend upon. Neither could the human species have survived throughout history without forming various groups: clans, families, communities, cities, states, and nations, to name a few. Out of this desire to belong, each of us develops the goal of making contact—physical or emotional—with other human beings. For an infant, physical contact, such as being held, is necessary for normal development and later helps the child gain a sense of belonging in the family. The self-esteem and courage that grow out of this sense of belonging make it possible for the child to connect to others outside the family. Schools, religious organizations, sports leagues, and other institutions offer additional opportunities for humans to achieve the goal of belonging.

During the teen years, friends often become more important than family, a fact that's tough for many parents to accept.

During the teen years, friends often become more important than family, a fact that's tough for many parents to accept. You may wonder, *Why would my teen rather just 'hang out' with the guys' than go with us to the park?* Because he knows, at least unconsciously, that a successful future depends on leaving the nest and belonging to other groups besides his family. Certainly family activities have a place in this process, but understand that at this stage in her life, your teen needs acceptance by peers more urgently than she needs acceptance by you. And that's not because she no longer likes you (no matter what she says); it's because she's feeling a natural desire to belong with other people.

Power

We'd all like to be able to influence our environment or at least gain a measure of control over it. We'd like for things to go our way; we want the power to make that happen. Teens, with their growing need for independence—and the reluctance of adults to give it to them, feel this desire for control and power very acutely.

Your teen will gain some power just by virtue of normal growth and development processes: she will grow physically from a child into a more powerful being who is not only bigger and stronger, but also is capable of reproducing other human beings. She will

Remember, if your teen is to successfully become an independent adult, she must have the power to leave you when the time is right.

also be intellectually more powerful, able to consider "what might be" as opposed to just "what is." It's natural for her to want to use these new skills in new ways. She may become critical of everything (including Mom and Dad), basking in the power her new intelligence gives her. Although teens who are trying out their new-found power are frustrating to live with, their experiments in empowerment are an important part of their transition from dependence to independence. Remember, if your teen is to successfully become an independent adult, she must have the power to leave you when the time is right.

Protection

To survive and thrive, we must be able to protect ourselves, our families, and our nation. Our instinct to repel attacks—whether physical or psychological—has led to the development of elaborate systems of justice and defense. Teens will also look for ways to protect themselves from physical harm or from threats to their self-esteem. But because they lack a mature understanding of justice and the interconnectedness of people, they often strike out in ways that are unproductive and even harmful. Parents and teachers can help teens learn responsible methods of protection while at the same time using adult resources to offer safe environments.

Remember, the goal of protection is normal for a teen. He's protecting the unique identity that he has worked hard to forge for himself. Partly because it's still a work in progress, a teen's emerging identity is especially vulnerable. If you try to force him to conform to your values or your way of doing things, he'll feel compelled to rebel in order to protect this identity. Instead, give him the message that "You don't have to be just like me; you just have to abide by certain rules." You can respect his point of view even when you disagree. You can also allow him some freedom in choosing things that let him express who he is: music, clothing, and hair style, for example. Even if, from your perspective of greater experience, you see these things as trivial, it's important to allow your teen the freedom to think otherwise—unless you see him becoming involved with a culture of negative values and behavior that he lacks the maturity to fully understand. We'll discuss how parents can be a filter in their teens' lives in Chapter 5.

Withdrawal

Time-outs are essential and refreshing in any sport. Just as a teen seeks contact, at other times he needs to withdraw, regroup, center. Withdrawal is a kind of counter-balancing act to the goal of belonging. The human survival instinct has also taught us to withdraw from danger.

Teens need time and privacy to sort out all the changes they're experiencing, to understand their new world and their place in it.

Spending more time alone in their bedrooms is usually normal behavior for teenagers. They need time and privacy to sort out all the changes they're experiencing, to understand their new world and their place in it. For the most part, you should allow them their privacy, with two exceptions: 1) if you suspect drug or alcohol use; and 2) if you think your teen is depressed. Too much withdrawal can be a signal that one of these major problems exists. In that case, you should get involved. In Chapters 5 and 6, you'll learn more about how to detect depression and prevent high-risk behavior.

Challenge

The four goals we have discussed begin early in childhood and continue throughout your teen's life. But the fifth goal, challenge, seems to emerge during adolescence. Your teen's desire to challenge himself—to test his skill and courage against an obstacle—is one way he measures how well he is doing on his journey from dependence to independence. It is a natural, age-old part of growing up. In fact, in many cultures teens have to endure a structured, traditional challenge to mark the transition from teen to adult. Because few teens in our culture must face the challenge of literal survival (thankfully), many create their own challenges by challenging their parents.

Positive and Negative Approaches to the Five Goals

An important aspect of these five basic goals is that they may be approached through either positive or negative behavior. The philosophy of Active Parenting is that there are no good or bad teens, only those who choose to pursue these basic goals in either positive or negative ways. Teens with high self-esteem and courage will generally choose the positive approaches. Those with low self-esteem and who are discouraged will more likely choose the easier, negative approaches. The following chart provides some labels we can use to distinguish these approaches:

How Teens Approach the Five Goals of Behavior		
Positive Approach	**Teen's Goal**	**Negative Approach**
Contributing	Belonging	Undue Attention-Seeking
Independence	Power	Rebellion
Assertiveness/Forgiveness	Protection	Revenge
Appropriate Avoidance	Withdrawal	Undue Avoidance
Safe Adventures	Challenge	Thrill-seeking

How to Determine a Teen's Goal

Because parents do not usually know the goals behind a teen's misbehavior, they often take an action that makes the problem worse.

Because parents do not usually know the goals behind a teen's misbehavior, they often take an action that makes the problem worse. In other words, the discipline actually pays off a teen's negative behavior by helping her achieve her goal. And if negative behavior works, why not continue to use it? After all, it's usually the easier approach.

The first step, then, is to determine what your teen really wants. Once you know her goal, you can help redirect her to choose a positive approach to getting it. This requires some detective work on your part. There are two clues that will usually tell you a teen's goal:

1. **Your own feeling during a conflict**

   Are you annoyed, angry, hurt, helpless or afraid? Because much of your teen's misbehavior is aimed at you, becoming aware of your own feelings during a conflict can be a powerful clue to her goals.

2. **The teen's response to your attempts at correcting the misbehavior**

   How does your teen behave after you've made an effort to correct the misbehavior?

The following chart is a guide for interpreting the answers to these two questions.

If you feel...	And your teen's response to correction is to...	Then your teen's goal is...	And the negative approach is...
Annoyed	stop the behavior, but start again very soon	Belonging	Undue Attention-Seeking
Angry	increase the misbehavior or give in only to fight again another day	Power	Rebellion
Hurt	continue to hurt you or increase the misbehavior	Protection	Revenge
Helpless	become passive; refuse to try	Withdrawal	Undue Avoidance
Unusually Afraid	take even more risks	Challenge	Thrill-seeking

Redirecting Your Teen's Behavior

The key to helping your teen shift from a negative to a positive approach with any of the five goals is to do the unexpected. You have to break the pattern the teen has come to expect, avoiding the payoffs that maintain their mistaken ideas. To see this more clearly, let's revisit the Think-Feel-Do Cycle.

Remember that teens respond to events in their lives in the order of the arrows: First, their thinking is triggered, including unconscious beliefs, values, and goals. It is here that the five basic goals operate. How the teen sees himself best achieving these goals in relation to an event produces a feeling. Then together the thinking and feeling, much of which is unconscious, produce a behavior. When the teen's thinking involves a negative approach to one of the five goals, the resulting behavior is a negative one. Let's take a closer look at how the five negative approaches work to achieve a teen's goal.

Negative Approach #1: Undue Attention-Seeking   *(Goal:* Belonging)

When a teen seeks to belong by taking the negative approach of undue attention-seeking, she may mistakenly believe that she must be the center of attention in order to belong. While children will more often do things to get this attention from *parents*, teens usually prefer the attention of *peers*. They may become class clowns or notorious troublemakers in their effort to stay in the limelight.

While peers may encourage such negative behavior, adults usually feel annoyed or irritated by it. When confronted by an adult, a teen will usually stop his negative behavior for a while, but will soon resume it. This makes sense when we consider that the teen's goal is to belong by staying noticed, and that by confronting the teen, a parent or other adult gives him that attention. This satisfies his desire for a while, but not for long.

How Parents Pay Off the Negative Approach of Undue Attention-Seeking:

Parents play into the hands of a teen seeking attention when they remind, nag, coax, complain, give lectures, scold, and otherwise stay in contact with the teen.

Anthony's mother usually worked too much to notice her son's comings and goings, but when Anthony started coming home later and later, she picked up on it. Then she began to notice other differences in the way Anthony dressed, the way he talked, his choice of friends… and when she saw that he'd drawn the insignia of a local gang on his school books, she started to fear for the worst. Sure enough, when confronted, Anthony confessed: he had joined a gang. From that point, his mother began to lecture him on a daily basis about the dangers of gang life. She still worked long hours, but now she felt like she had to make time to talk to him. She nagged him whenever they were together, and they spent most of that time in a shouting match, but that was fine with Anthony. He was getting what he wanted: a sense of belonging from his new gang, plus undue attention from his mother for doing something that she didn't approve of. Her lecturing, although unpleasant, was the most contact he'd had with her in years.

Teens who seek the goal of belonging through the negative approach of undue attention seeking might be unconsciously thinking, "I must be noticed to be OK." Their low self-esteem produces a feeling of anxiety and discouragement. To eliminate these unpleasant feelings, they choose an annoying or controversial behavior that gets them the attention they crave. Each time a parent reminds, nags, lectures, or corrects, the teen subconsciously thinks, "Yes, she noticed me again and I'm OK." He'll feel better, temporarily, but soon will need another dose of undue attention to keep feeling OK.

What can you do to avoid paying off this negative approach?

- Act more and talk less.

- When you must discipline, briefly confront your teen with an "I" message or a logical consequence.

- Help your teen achieve the recognition and contact she wants by playing a useful role. Help find meaningful ways for her to contribute to the family while ignoring some of her unproductive attention-getting behavior.

Let's see how Anthony's mom broke the cycle…

One day when Anthony's mother complained to herself for the thousandth time, *Why does my son do this to me?!* she realized that she knew the answer: Because my nagging is a "pay off" for his negative behavior. Understanding that Anthony's goal was to belong—something that was missing from their family, since she was always working and he'd never known his father—she decided to change tactics. So she stopped nagging and yelling and she spoke to the youth director at her church. Anthony had always enjoyed basketball but hadn't played much in the past couple of years. She convinced him to join a church league and even made time to go to some of the games herself. After each game, she made him a special dinner, which the two enjoyed together. In this way, she began to loosen the hold Anthony's gang had on him. She felt confident that in time Anthony would lose interest in the gang altogether.

Negative Approach #2: Rebellion   *(Goal:* Power*)*

Rebellion is the most common of the five negative approaches that teens use, and it's the one that causes the most conflict in families and schools throughout the world. The teen who becomes discouraged trying to gain power in positive ways can easily find power through rebellion. After all, in any power struggle,

> *The person in position to say "no" is in the more powerful position.*

If parents have an autocratic leadership style, their teen may justly feel that his natural movement toward independence has been wrongly stifled. A teen with strong self-esteem and courage will stand up to his parents and negotiate for more freedom. But if the teen is already discouraged and lacking self-esteem, he may simply rebel through negative behavior.

Rebellious teens mistakenly believe the only way they can achieve power is by controlling others, or at least by showing others they cannot be controlled by them.

How Parents Pay Off the Negative Approach of Rebellion:

You'll know you're in a power struggle when you frequently get angry at your teen. When you express this anger aggressively by yelling, lashing out with threats and punishments, and otherwise "losing control," you are joining in the power struggle. The more you try to overpower your teen, the more she resists. Why? Because she has learned that you may eventually give in, in which case she wins. And even if you don't give in, the mere fact that she has engaged you in a fight and made you angry has the payoff of confirming that she really is powerful.

When Nicole's parents told her that she couldn't go to the mall if Devon and his friends were going to be there, Nicole flew into a rage. "You can't control my life!" she screamed. Mr. and Mrs. Lewis had good reasons for their request—Devon had a reputation for being wild and rebellious—but Nicole's anger was infectious. Soon all three of them were shouting at each other, and the opportunity for a reasonable discussion was lost. The power struggle raged until, finally, Mr. Lewis hit his limit and flipped into Dictator mode: "That's enough from you, young lady," he announced. "You're grounded. You're not going to the mall or anywhere else for two weeks."

When you fight with your teen, you are saying to her, "Look how powerful you are: You've made me angry and pulled me down to your level."

What can you do to avoid paying off this negative approach?

- Refuse to fight or give in, and you'll side-step the struggle for power.

- Take your sail out of your teen's wind. In other words, call a "time out" and excuse yourself until you both calm down.

- Express more confidence in your teen's ability to make decisions for herself. Let her make mistakes and experience the consequences without lecturing or humiliating her.

- Hold family meetings to involve your teen in making decisions that affect the whole family.

- Use family enrichment activities, communication skills, and methods of encouragement to begin winning a more cooperative relationship with your teen.

- Use the FLAC Method to defuse the power struggle and set consequences when necessary.

- Learn to use your own anger positively.

Despite being grounded, Nicole had found a way to meet Devon at the mall the next day. This had given Mr. and Mrs. Lewis pause; maybe yelling and grounding their daughter were only making matters worse. The more they tried to control her, the more she rebelled. They asked Nicole to sit down and discuss the problem together. This time, they decided beforehand not to fight with her, but also not to give in to her demands. "You know, Nicole," they began, "Maybe there's room for us to back off a little without giving up our responsibility as parents." Nicole was pleased that her parents were finally paying attention to her feelings. She agreed to try solving problems together. As they began to come up with guidelines that they all could live with, Mr. and Mrs. Lewis made sure they focused on Nicole's strengths and avoided the discouraging comments they had made in the past. They knew that there would be other power struggles, but everyone felt encouraged that they had taken an important first step.

Negative Approach #3: Revenge   *(Goal:* Protection*)*

Power struggles can often result in a teen wanting revenge, especially if he feels that his parents have "won too many battles" or have hurt him. He may decide that the best form of protection is to hurt back. In response, parents often retaliate with punishment, thus setting off an escalating revenge cycle. You can never win this revenge war. All the teen has to do to hurt you is to fail. He can fail any number of ways: at school, with his peers, with drugs, with unsafe sex. In extreme cases, he can fail at life by committing suicide.

How Parents Pay Off the Negative Approach of Revenge:

When teens seek to protect themselves by getting revenge, they are usually feeling very discouraged. The typical retaliation from parents—punishment and put-downs—

discourages them further and confirms their belief that they have a right to hurt their parents back.

> Tina's pregnancy had hurt her father fiercely, which is exactly what she wanted—unconsciously, that is. For all the times he had hurt her, this was the ultimate slap in his face. On some level, Tina's father understood this, and it made him so angry that his instinct was to hurt her some more. He wanted to call her a "stupid slut" and throw her out of the house.

The more we hurt our teens, the more they want to hurt us back. And the revenge cycle continues.

What can you do to avoid paying off this negative approach?

- Stop the revenge cycle. Instead of stubbornly demanding that your teen change (which is what many of us have been taught to do), play the leadership role in the family and call a cease-fire.

- Remember that no teen is born "bad" or "mean." When teens act in a bad or mean way, they are hurting inside. Do what you can to stop whatever is hurting the teen. If it's your behavior, take a new approach. If someone else is hurting her, support her while she handles it herself, or take more direct action if needed.

- Sometimes a vengeful teen is hurting because he has a misconception about how life ought to work. Frank communication is the way to go.

- The FLAC method and other skills for handling a power struggle can be useful in redirecting a revenge-seeking teen.

- Work on strengthening your relationship with family enrichment activities, active communication, encouragement, and other support skills.

> Tina's father stopped himself before the poisonous words could come out. He took a deep breath and paused to think. Then, with great effort, he rose above his anger and indignation. Maybe he was part of the problem. Regardless, it was time for a cease-fire. Tina was surprised when her father invited her to sit down with him and then told her that no matter what happened, she was his daughter and that he loved her and wanted to help her through this.

Negative Approach #4: Undue Avoidance *(Goal:* Withdrawal)

Most teenagers go through times when they withdraw from friends and family into their own thoughts and feelings. This self-reflection may be anxiety-ridden and full of doubt, but it is a normal part of development. You'll know your teen has crossed the line into undue avoidance when his behavior becomes a substitute for facing life's problems.

Teenagers who become discouraged may sink so low in self-esteem that they give up trying altogether. These teens can slip into a state of depression and even think of suicide as a solution to their problems. Their belief becomes, "I can't succeed, so I'll stop trying. Then I won't have to worry about failure." They develop an apathy and lack of motivation that often leave parents feeling helpless. School performance may decline when they start to skip classes, fail to complete assignments, or even drop out. Alcohol and other drugs may become a way for those teens to avoid the challenges that life poses and to find temporary relief from their own discouragement. We will talk more about teen depression and suicide in Chapter 5.

How Parents Pay Off the Negative Approach of Avoidance:

Parents often make the mistake of giving up on a teen who has taken the approach of avoidance. They write him off as a loser and stop making an effort to help, or they yell and scream, humiliate, and punish. Either way, they send the message that "You're not good enough for us." This confirms the teen's own evaluation of himself and so justifies his avoidance of life's problems.

After yet another straight-F report card to top off months of screaming matches with his parents, Jamal grew so discouraged with his failures at school that finally he gave up altogether and dropped out. His parents threw up their hands in defeat, accepting that their son had lost his ambition. *See,* Jamal told himself, *Even my parents think I'm a worthless loser. There's no point in trying to be anything else.*

What can you do to avoid paying off this negative approach?

- Communicate to your teen that succeed or fail, win or lose, you are glad that she is your child. Your love is unconditional.

- Practice patience and offer a lot of encouragement.

- Remind yourself that your teen may be exaggerating his avoidance to gauge your reaction. He may want to determine if the worst is true—if he is really as bad off as he thinks.

- Help your teen find tasks at which she can succeed, which will help her gain confidence and improve her self-image.

- Use the BANK Method to encourage success.

- Help your teen see that mistakes are for learning and that failure is just a lesson on the road to success.

- Get him extra help if he needs it, including professional evaluation and counseling, if you think necessary.

After a talk with a counselor, Jamal's parents decided this should not be the end of the story for them or their son. Maybe a break from school would do Jamal some good. They sat down with him to discuss his future. Everyone agreed that he should take a job and work through the end of the semester and then reevaluate the situation. In the meantime, since he was no longer a student, he would be expected to help pay his own expenses. His parents expressed confidence that he would make a good life for himself whatever path he ultimately decided to take.

Negative Approach #5: **Thrill Seeking**   *(Goal:* **Challenge)**

Excitement is to teens as comfort and stability is to us adults. In fact, if it weren't for teens and preteens, there would be little need for roller coasters or horror movies. After years of development, teens are ready to challenge themselves physically, emotionally, intellectually, socially, and spiritually. If the world does not offer them healthy ways to do this, they'll find plenty of unhealthy ways. Alcohol and drugs, sexual experimentation, reckless driving, and breaking the law can be thrilling alternatives to a teen who sees everyday life as bland. For teens who are also choosing undue avoidance, thrill-seeking may become the only thing they feel they are good at. "If I can't be the best student," the thinking sometimes goes, "then at least I can be the biggest druggie." Danger is entertaining and exciting.

You'll know your teen is using the negative approach of thrill-seeking if you're unusually afraid for your teen when he misbehaves and if, when you discipline him, he responds by taking even more reckless risks.

How Parents Pay Off the Negative Approach of Thrill-Seeking:

If you are an overprotective parent who does not allow your teen to take *any* risks—even reasonable ones—you inadvertently heighten the appeal of thrill-seeking to your teen. Teens have a legitimate need to test themselves. When you try to stifle this desire, it often becomes stronger. Parents also err by reacting with anger and outrage when they find teens drinking or engaging in other harmful thrill-seeking behavior. This response often turns thrill-seeking into a power struggle. The teen now has two motivations to continue: the thrill itself and to show Mom and Dad that they can't run his life.

> Diane was bored with life in her little town. She didn't understand how anyone could stand such a dull existence without something to spice it up. Diane had started smoking marijuana at age 13 and by 15 was doing crystal meth. She had also gotten into the thrill seeking of promiscuous sex and shoplifting. Danger gave her a sense of mastery and excitement that she couldn't get anywhere else. Her parents constantly nagged and warned her that she'd end up dead or in jail, but if anything, this made Diane behave even more recklessly.

What can you do to avoid paying off this negative approach?

- Avoid power struggles. During confrontations, remain calm and use a firm tone of voice.

- Redirect your teen toward activities that are challenging but not irresponsible or overly dangerous (often because they are adult-supervised), such as karate, rock climbing, white-water sports, team sports, volunteering, a part-time job, a hobby, or an outdoor adventure program like Outward Bound.

- Help your teen enjoy vicarious thrills by taking him to sporting events, performances, and other exciting spectacles.

- Double the benefits by learning something together.

- Of course, you'll want to confront and discipline reckless behavior, but it will benefit everyone involved if you look for more creative ways to help teens challenge themselves. This will eliminate much of the problem.

One night, while shoplifting with some friends and high on a cocktail of different drugs, Diane got caught by security and was arrested. This ended up being the best thing that could have happened to her at this point in her life. Fortunately for her, her parents and the judge helped her get into a drug treatment program where she began to look at the consequences of her choices in life. Family therapy was part of the process, as her parents discovered ways to help her build her self-esteem and courage and to find healthy ways to challenge herself.

The following chart provides an overview of the five goals of teen behavior, how and why teens approach these goals, and the best role for parents in each set of circumstances.

Basic Goal of Teen's Action	Teen's Approach to Goal	Teen's Belief	Parent's Typical Feeling	Teen's Response to Correction	Parent's Role
Belonging	Contribution *(Positive)*	My contributions are recognized. I earn belonging by cooperating.			Encourage cooperation, acknowledge the teen's contributions.
	Undue Attention-Seeking *(Negative)*	I belong only when I'm noticed or served. The world must revolve around me.	Annoyance	Stops, but begins again very soon	Ignore the behavior. Give the child full attention other times. Use consequences. Act more; talk less.

Chart continued on the next page...

Basic Goal of Teen's Action	Teen's Approach to Goal	Teen's Belief	Parent's Typical Feeling	Teen's Response to Correction	How to Redirect
Power	Independence *(Positive)*	I am able to influence what happens to me. I am responsible for my life.			Give responsibilities. Continue to encourage.
	Rebellion *(Negative)*	I feel OK only when I'm the boss or when I'm showing you that you can't boss me.	Anger	Escalates behavior or gives in only to fight again another day	Remove yourself from the conflict. Talk after cooling off. Don't fight or give in. Use FLAC.
Protection	Assertiveness, Forgiveness *(Positive)*	I can stand up for myself and those I love. I am able to forgive and move on.			Express positive feelings. Be assertive and forgive in your own relationships.
	Revenge *(Negative)*	I've been hurt and will get even by hurting back.	Hurt	Continues to lash out or escalates misbehavior	Refuse to be hurt. Withdraw from the conflict. Show love. Avoid temptation to hurt back. Use FLAC.
Withdrawal	Appropriate Avoidance *(Positive)*	There are times when I need to be alone and situations in which I should be left alone.			Respect teen's wishes to be alone. Don't press. Later, use Active Communication.
	Avoidance *(Negative)*	I'm a failure at everything. Leave me alone. Expect nothing from me.	Helplessness	Is passive; refuses to try; gives up	Be patient; find ways to encourage. Build skills using BANK.
Challenge	Safe Adventures *(Positive)*	I enjoy a good challenge, as long as it's reasonably safe.			Support and encourage healthy challenging activities.
	Thrill-Seeking *(Negative)*	I just want the excitement and don't care about the risks.	Unusually afraid for your teen	Takes even greater risks	Avoid anger; Use respectful discipline; Find safer challenges

Family Meeting: Problem-Prevention Talks

Teens often misbehave simply because they don't know what parents expect from them. They don't know where the limits are and how much freedom they are allowed. Of course, many a shrewd teen will intentionally stay in the dark about the rules, operating on the belief that "it's easier to gain forgiveness than permission." In either case, many problems can be prevented if you take the time to discuss guidelines and expectations before the situation occurs.

As you certainly know by now, the Active Parenting approach to problem prevention is not about laying down the law or telling your teen what the rules are. You will find that you can be much more effective at parenting if you discuss potential problems with your teen and decide together what solution or guidelines the situation requires. Of course, as the parent you will have certain limits that are non-negotiable, but a willingness to be flexible within those limits can go a long way to winning cooperation and avoiding problems.

For example:

> *Your teen wants to go to a party. You're concerned about alcohol and other drug use. Talking with her before the party can reduce the risks of her getting involved with drugs.*

Follow these guidelines to make your Problem-Prevention Talk most effective:

> ### Guidelines for Problem-Prevention Talks
>
> 1. Identify potential problems and risks.
>
> 2. Share thoughts and feelings.
>
> 3. Generate guidelines for behavior.
>
> 4. Decide on logical consequences for violating the guidelines (if necessary).
>
> 5. Follow up later.

Let's go over them one by one.

1. Identify potential problems and risks.

If you have been in similar situations before, then you probably know where the trouble spots will be. Otherwise, use your experience of similar situations and your knowledge of your teen to anticipate the problems.

For example:

"You know how strongly we feel that you not use tobacco, alcohol, or other drugs. So, for us to feel good about your going to this or other parties, we need to be clear about some things. "

2. Share thoughts and feelings.

Ask your teen what he thinks about the situation and what problems might arise. You may be surprised that he also has concerns. Then make clear your own thoughts and feelings in a friendly manner.

For example:

"We want to reduce the chance that someone pressures you to use drugs, which means not being around kids who are using them."

3. **Generate guidelines for behavior**.

   Using the information you gathered in step two, talk with your teen about what you expect of him. When discussing guidelines, keep in mind that it will be easier for your teen to comply with the rules if he feels like he is gaining something by doing so. We aren't suggesting the use of rewards or bribes for cooperative behavior, but including incentives can be effective.

   For example:

   > *"So, we agree that if anyone at the party is using alcohol or other drugs, you'll call us to pick you up. That way, we'll feel OK about your going to other parties."*

4. **Decide on logical consequences for violating the guidelines (if necessary)**.

   Your teen will be more likely to follow the guidelines if he knows what will happen if he violates one. You don't need to use this step with kids who are basically cooperative or who have not had problems in similar situations. In fact, such a warning may seem like an insult to a teen who only needs to be included in the discussion and have his needs considered in order to cooperate. For more challenging kids, however, consequences are very helpful when done right.

   For example:

   > *"So, to be clear, if you want to continue going to parties, you need to make sure that you only stay at a party if it's free of drugs and alcohol."*

5. **Follow up later**.

   In situations where you are not around to ensure that your teen followed the guidelines, you will need to find a way to see how your teen behaved, such as by speaking to an adult who was there. If your teen has followed the guidelines, you can encourage her by acknowledging the good effort. If she has not, then you will need to enforce the logical consequences.

   For example:

   > *"I spoke to Mr. Peterson the other day, and he said that the party at his home went very well. I asked him about drinking and stuff, and he said that they had enough adults there to make sure everything was OK, and that you guys had a great time and didn't cause any trouble."*

Family Enrichment Activity: Teaching Skills

Two of the main concepts we've covered in this chapter have been encouragement and power. An important part of your job as a parent is to encourage the development of courage, self-esteem and other positive traits and values in your teen. You are also challenged to empower your teen to succeed and to avoid those frustrating power struggles. The family enrichment activity for this chapter is to teach your teen a skill—something that he wants to learn. There is something to the saying that "knowledge is power." A teen achieves power through the positive approach of skill mastery, and thus he will have less need to rebel. And since you are the one empowering him, this activity has the double benefit of strengthening your relationship.

The tips on the next page can help you teach a skill effectively.

Tips for Teaching Skills

1. **Motivate**. Encourage your teen to want to learn the skill by explaining the value it has to him or to the entire family. Increase motivation by making the skill as relevant to his life as possible. For example:

    > *"When I teach you how to change the oil yourself,*
    > *you'll save a lot of money."*

2. **Select a good time**. Pick a time when neither you nor your teen will be rushed or interrupted.

3. **Break the skill down into small steps**. This makes it much easier to learn. When skills are learned one step at a time, there are more successes to help build courage and motivation. For example:

    > *"The first step in making our family's secret lasagna recipe is to take*
    > *out the 9 x 12-inch baking pan and all the ingredients."*

4. **Demonstrate**. When teaching a difficult skill, it's helpful to demonstrate the skill yourself (provided you can do it!), explaining slowly as you do:

    > *"Let me show you my famous over-and-under move. First, you drive to the basket*
    > *like this. Then you start up like you're going for a lay-up, like this. Then…"*

5. **Let your teen try**. Let her perform the skill while you stand by, ready to offer help if she needs it. Be gentle about mistakes, and keep a sense of humor. For example:

    > *"Okay, now you try it. Just take it slow and steady, and*
    > *if you see a flashing blue light, pull over."*

6. **Encourage, encourage, encourage**. Make plenty of encouraging comments that acknowledge your teen's efforts as well as results. This builds self-esteem and keeps his motivation high to continue learning. For example:

    > *"Great! That's the way to do it."*

7. **Work or play together**. Once your teen has learned the skill to an appropriate level, you can sometimes work or play together, so that you can both enjoy the companionship of the activity. For example:

    > *"OK, let's go play a round of golf!"*

chapter **4**

Home Activities

1. Practice encouraging (and avoiding discouraging) your teen, using the four types of encouragement. Complete the Encouragement Profile on page 159. It will help you start thinking in an encouraging way. Then complete the guide sheets on pages 157-158 to improve your understanding of the four methods of encouragement.

2. Work on understanding the five goals of teen behavior. Learn to identify which goals motivate your teen and how to avoid "paying off" the misbehavior. The guide sheet on page 160 will help you.

3. Choose a potential problem, and have a family meeting using the Problem Prevention Talks model to address it with your family.

4. For your family enrichment activity, teach a skill to your teen. Complete the guide sheet on page 161.

Encouragement Video Practice

Example #1 Matt and Mom: Discouraging

If you were Matt, what would you be thinking?	What would you be feeling?	What will you do next?	What discouraging influence(s) did Mom use?

Example #1 Matt and Mom: Encouraging

Example #2 Jada and Dad: Discouraging

If you were Jada, what would you be thinking?	What would you be feeling?	What will you do next?	What discouraging influence(s) did Dad use?

Example #2 Jada and Dad: Encouraging

Example #3 Erin and Stepmom: Discouraging

If you were Erin, what would you be thinking?	What would you be feeling?	What will you do next?	What discouraging influence(s) did Stepmom use?

Example #3 Erin and Stepmom: Encouraging

This guide sheet refers to the Active Parenting of Teens *discussion program. If you are using this Parent's Guide independently and are interested in participating in a discussion group, check out our web site for information:* www.ActiveParenting.com/ParentingTeens

156

Turning Discouragement into Encouragement

Practice the four methods of building encouragement with your teen.

Stimulating Independence

Think of three tasks that you are currently doing for your teen that she could do for herself.

1. _____

2. _____

3. _____

Now choose at least one of these tasks to let your teen do for herself this week. Don't forget to encourage!

Building on Strengths

Identify a goal for your teen and use the BANK method to help him achieve it.

Goal: _____

Baby steps: Break the process into three steps. 1. 2. 3.	Acknowledge what your teen already does well that will help him achieve the goal. Write it here.
Nudge your teen to take the next step. What can you say to do this in an encouraging way?	Keep encouraging improvement. What words of encouragement can you use?

Cnntinued on the next page...

Turning Discouragement into Encouragement (continued)

Showing Confidence

Find ways to encourage your teen by showing confidence in one or more of the methods below.

1. What **responsibility** did you give your teen? _____

_____

2. What did you **ask your teen's advice or opinion** about? _____

_____

3. When did you **avoid the temptation to rescue or take over** for your teen? _____

_____

Valuing Your Teen As-Is

Find ways to show that you value your teen for who he is, using some of the methods below.

1. Name one way that you **separated your teen's worth from his accomplishments**. _____

_____

2. Name one way that you **separated your teen's worth from his misbehavior**. _____

_____

3. Name at least one way that you **appreciated your teen's uniqueness**. _____

_____

Encouragement Profile

Everyone has abilities, talents, and positive qualities. Think about these qualities in your teen and yourself and write some below, filling in names as you go.

_____ does well at _____

_____ .

I do well at _____ .

_____ helps me _____

_____ .

I help _____ with _____

_____ .

_____ is learning _____

_____ .

I am learning _____ .

A strength _____ has is _____

_____ .

One of my strengths is _____

_____ .

_____ learned how to _____

_____ .

What I like best about _____ is _____

_____ .

What I like best about myself is _____

_____ .

Identifying the Negative Approach

The following questions will help to give you a better understanding of the five goals of teen behavior, your teen's approach to the goals, and whether you are paying off your teen's misbehavior.

Describe a recent conflict that you had with your teen. _____

_____

How did you feel during the exchange (irritated, angry, hurt, hopeless, afraid)? _____

_____

How did your teen respond to your attempts to correct him? _____

_____

_____

Using the chart on pages 148-149 , what was your teen's negative approach? _____

_____

What was your teen's basic goal? _____

How did you mistakenly pay off the negative approach? _____

_____

_____

What will you do differently next time? _____

_____

_____

Family Enrichment Activity: Teaching Skills

Remember when...

Think about a skill that one of your parents taught you. Try to visualize the experience.

What was the skill that your parents taught you? _____

How did you feel about your parent at that time? _____

How did you feel about yourself? _____

What mistakes did your parent make that you could avoid? _____

_____

What positive things did your parent do that you could do, too? _____

_____

Plan the Lesson

Pick an activity you'd like to work on with your teen, such as:

- a sport skill
- opening a bank account
- saying "no" to someone without looking like a jerk
- something to do with the car
- cooking a special dish

Talk it over with your teen first, then list here the skills you will teach:

_____

_____

Teach the Skill and Report the Results

Refer to the seven steps on page 154 as you teach the skill. Afterwards, answer these questions:

What went well? _____

_____

What might you do better next time? _____

_____

Drugs, Sexuality, and Violence: Reducing the Risks

Part 1

On April 10, 1912, the steamship *Titanic* set off on its maiden voyage from England for New York. By all accounts, it was the safest ship ever built. Five days after embarking, the captain received a telegram warning that a dangerous ice field lay ahead. He had plenty of time to slow the engines, change his course, and avoid risking a disaster. However, he mistakenly thought that he could save time by steering around any icebergs in his path. When a giant iceberg loomed ahead, he thought the ship could slide past. The officer did manage to steer around the portion of the iceberg that was visible above water, but not around the other seven-eighths of it that extended beneath the surface. It was this underwater portion of the iceberg that ripped through the *Titanic's* hull like a can opener. The officer's mistake cost him his life as well as the lives of 1,523 others who went down with the ship.

Teens often approach problems just as the *Titanic* officer approached the iceberg: They think they know the risks of such ventures as drinking, drug use, sex, and violence; They also mistakenly believe that they can steer around those risks and slide by unharmed. But like the officer on the Titanic, teens often fail to see the bulk of the danger—addiction, STDs, pregnancy (and parenthood), accidents, criminal records, prison, death. Like the *Titanic*, which was built to be strong and safe, they may have plenty of ballast—courage, responsibility, self-esteem, and other valuable character traits— to stay afloat in a storm, but one mistake in judgment can be deadly. Part of a parent's job is to help teach them about the risks and get them to slow down their engines.

Many teens are misinformed about the true risks of drug use, unsafe sex, and violence. But many others are well aware of what can happen from a single overdose, a drunk driving accident, an HIV infection, or a serious fight. Why, then, do they get involved? Often it's because they mistakenly believe they can get around the dangers and escape unharmed, just as the *Titanic* officer believed he could get around the iceberg without cutting the engines. "It won't happen to me" is an almost universal thought among teens. They feel they are invincible. Also, let's face it, experimenting with drugs and sex—even violence—can be enjoyable and exciting. Media images and music often reinforce the glamour.

Drugs, Sexuality, and Violence: The Think-Feel-Do Cycle

While no teenager is immune from the lure of drugs, sexuality, and violence, troubled teenagers are even more vulnerable. A teen with low self-esteem is in a prime position to lose himself in the pleasure or excitement of drugs, sexuality, or violence and so escape the pain and insecurity of self-doubt.

Let's consider the Think-Feel-Do Cycle again. Imagine the typical failure cycle of a teen boy who is shy around girls and hasn't the confidence or skills to approach them. He's at a party and is offered a beer.

Read the cycle clockwise, one number at a time.

EVENT
1. At party; offered beer
5. Drinking with the group

THINK
2. "Sure. Everyone else is drinking."
6. "This is cool. Maybe I'll have another."

FEEL
3. Relieved to be fitting in
7. A little drunk, and less self-conscious around girls

DO
4. He drinks a beer.
8. Laughing and having fun... and having another beer.

We've all heard of alcohol giving a person "courage." This allows the drinker a short cut instead of developing real skills (in this case, social skills) and real courage. But to maintain the illusion, he has to keep getting drunk or even getting high on other drugs. This is where addiction starts. As the teen relies more and more on alcohol or drugs, crucial opportunities to develop social and emotional skills are lost.

The same thing can happen with sex. The pleasure and thrill of sex helps many teenagers temporarily forget their problems. Or teens may turn to sex for any number of misguided purposes: to boost confidence, to make them feel socially acceptable, to rebel against parental or other adult authority, as a substitute for more difficult ways to get to know one another, and the list goes on. Once a teen starts using sex as a short cut to temporary success, it becomes increasingly difficult for him to achieve his goals without it.

The skills and strategies presented in this chapter are critical to the prevention of alcohol and drug abuse, unhealthy sexual activity, and violence in your teen's life. The more you help your teen build a strong sense of self-esteem and courage, the less tempting these dangerous activities become.

Teen Depression and Suicide

Depression is a serious condition that affects anywhere from 4% of teens (severe depression) to 20% (mild to moderate depression). Teens suffering from depression have become so discouraged trying to cope with mounting pressures and the confusion of growing towards independence that they experience a persistent mood change resulting in overwhelming feelings of sadness, despair, or anger. They see no hope for happiness or success, and as a result their chances of achieving happiness and success are greatly diminished. Left untreated, depression can escalate into problems at school, home, and even in the community, including drug use as a means of self-medicating the problem, or suicide and other forms of violence to one's self and to others.

Though depression is a highly treatable condition, too many parents miss the warning signs or misread depression as just another phase of adolescence. Depression is more than a prolonged bout of moodiness or sadness. Look for some of these symptoms:

- Persistent sadness or hopelessness
- Irritability, anger, or hostility
- Frequent crying
- Apathy (not caring)
- Withdrawal from most friends or family
- Loss of interest in friends or activities
- Negative changes in eating or sleeping habits
- Restlessness and agitation
- Lack of energy
- Feelings of worthlessness or guilt
- Difficulty concentrating
- Unexplained aches and pains
- Extreme sensitivity to criticism
- Mentions of suicide or death

The more of these symptoms that are present in a teen and the longer they have lasted, the more likely the teen is depressed. If you see a number of these signs, use the communication skills presented in Chapter 2 to talk with your teen about how she is feeling and what is upsetting her. Be gently persistent, and expect some denial. If there is a particular problem that is triggering the depression, you may be able to support your teen in finding a solution. However, if the depression seems deep or more general, set up an appointment for an evaluation with your family physician or a mental health professional who specializes in adolescents.

Suicide is the third leading cause of death among 15- to 24-year-olds, according to research from the CDC (Centers for Disease Control), despite the fact that a large majority of suicide attempts are not successful. Why are suicide attempts so common among teens? Like any problem behavior, a suicide attempt may be a means to achieving any of the five goals of behavior. However, it is most often associated with one of these three:

Goal	Negative Approach	Beliefs (often unconscious)
Belonging	Undue attention seeking	*Maybe somebody will see how badly I am hurting and do something to help me* (a so-called "cry for help")
Protection	Revenge	*After I'm gone, they'll be sorry about how bad they treated me!*
Withdrawal	Avoidance	*It's hopeless. Life is not worth living anymore.*

In addition to the signs of depression, the following warning signs indicate a risk of suicide:

- Talking or even joking about committing suicide
- Expressions of hopelessness: "I might as well be dead."
- Glorifying death: "I bet people will remember me after I'm gone."
- Having a lot of accidents or engaging in reckless behavior
- Giving away favorite possessions (preparing for death)
- Saying goodbye to friends and family
- Seeking out weapons, pills, or other ways to commit suicide

If you find yourself in an emergency situation where your teen is threatening to commit suicide, call a suicide hotline or 911. In a non-emergency situation, such as if you detect signs of depression in your teen, contact your family physician or a mental health professional. You can be a big part of the solution, but don't try to do it all by yourself.

Ten Prevention Strategies for Parents

Preventing your teen from becoming harmfully involved with drugs, sexuality, and violence is one of the greatest gifts you can give. In fact, it can often be as precious as life itself. Like all of parenting, prevention is not an absolute science; it is a matter of probabilities. If you take the steps recommended in this chapter and the next you will improve the chances that your teen will make good choices regarding these risks. However, parents do not control their teens behavior 100%. I have emphasized that our role is to influence, not control. In spite of their best efforts, many excellent parents have seen their teens make poor decisions regarding drugs, sexuality and violence. But since the chances of your teen remaining safe improve as your knowledge, skills, and involvement improve, the odds are in favor of teens whose parents make the time and effort to take preventative action.

Building a good relationship with your teen is the first step in the prevention process. Without this relationship, your words and actions are unlikely to be effective and may even be counter-productive.

Building a good relationship with your teen is the first step in the prevention process. Without this relationship, your words and actions are unlikely to be effective and may even be counter-productive. Hopefully, the skills you have already learned in this book have helped you improve this relationship. The second step is to help your teen build the character to face life's challenges head-on, without resorting to drugs and other quick fixes. The skills of discipline, communication, and problem solving continue to play a key role in this process.

In this chapter and the next we will build on this base as we apply ten specific strategies for preventing teens' harmful use of drugs, sexuality, and violence. These ten strategies are derived from work I did on a panel of thirty experts from around the country assembled by the U.S. Office of Substance Abuse Prevention (OSAP)[1]. The project was called "Parenting Is Prevention," and its results continue to emphasize the importance of skilled parental involvement in the prevention process.

The strategies we cover in this chapter will focus on issues around sexuality, although you can apply the strategies to any behavior that is risky for your teen.

---

1 Now called CSAP (Center for Substance Abuse Prevention).

Strategy #1. Be a positive role model and teacher of values.

Your teen is just now learning how to act like an adult. Because adult decisions and choices are new to him, he needs values and beliefs that he can base his actions on when he's not sure what to do. As the most important person in your teen's life, you can help him form these values by talking with him about issues and setting a good example yourself.

Imagine that you and your teen are watching a movie together when one of the characters lights up a cigarette. This is a great opportunity to influence your teen. You could say, "How can they show cigarette smoking looking so cool when it's killing this guy? It wouldn't look cool if they flashed ahead twenty years to when he's dying in pain from cancer." Without directly confronting your teen, you have given him something to think about. You can also have a family talk later and present more evidence of the harmful effects of tobacco. See "Family Talks" on page 173 for some guidelines.

What you do is a much stronger indicator of your values than what you say. So ask yourself: What do I model for my teen through my behavior? Do I "walk my talk"?

Of course your words would ring hollow with your teen if two minutes later you lit up a cigarette yourself. You are your teen's role model. What you do is a much stronger indicator of your values than what you say. So ask yourself: *What do I model for my teen through my behavior? Do I "walk my talk"?* As the saying goes: "Values aren't taught; they're caught." What you teach your teen about risky behaviors—the use of tobacco, alcohol, and other drugs, sexual activity, and violence—is as much about your own behavior as is it about what you say you value.

- If a parent engages in unsafe or unhealthy behavior, a teen learns it isn't important to avoid temptation and high risk behavior.

- If a parent uses illegal substances, a teen learns that it's not important to abide by the law. If the parent can sneak, the teen concludes that she can sneak, too.

169

■ If a father treats women as sexual objects, making crude and sexist comments, the teen concludes that women are not worthy of respect.

■ If a parent flies off the handle in rage when things don't go her way, the teen learns to use intimidation to bully people into giving in.

■ If a parent gets drunk, the teen believes that it's okay to use alcohol without limits.

On the other hand:

■ If a parent resists some desires in order to stay safe and healthy, a teen learns that saying "no" is sometimes necessary.

■ If a parent follows the law and expresses disapproval of a TV or movie character who breaks the law, the teen learns that laws (and rules) are to be obeyed.

■ If a father treats women respectfully, avoiding crude remarks and expressing disapproval when other men make such remarks, the teen learns that men should treat women with respect.

■ If a parent is patient and uses peaceful methods to resolve conflicts, the teen learns to manage anger effectively and solve problems without violence.

■ If a parent drinks in moderation and discusses why adults can but teens can't, the teen learns how to be a responsible drinker and to stay within the law. Of course, if parents choose to refrain from all drinking, they will model abstinence to their teens.

■ If a parent's behavior is in line with what the parent says she values, the teen learns that the parent has integrity and will value her opinions and advice because the teen knows they are backed up by the parent's actions.

Sometimes parents aren't aware that their actions conflict with the values they are trying to teach their teens. If you take the time to examine your own habits and behaviors, you can get a better picture of what your teen sees when she observes you and whether you need to change anything you *do* to make it match what you *say*. The *Parent Role-Model Questionnaire* on page 192 will help you get started.

Parenting and Sexual Orientation

Attitudes and values about sexuality are constantly changing. In biblical days, polygamy was accepted as status quo, while today it is forbidden by law and rejected by most religions. As late as the 1970s homosexuality was listed as a mental disorder by the American Psychological Association, and now it is not. Today the gay, lesbian, bisexual, and transgender (GLBT) community is increasingly visible and accepted as a healthy part of society. This is not to say that the subject is not still controversial. Prejudice and discrimination can cause problems for the children of GLBT parents and for GLBT children and teens.

If you are a GLBT parent, use the skills you've learned in this program to communicate effectively with your children about their feelings and the issues they encounter because their parents are not of the traditional mold. If you are the heterosexual parent of a teen who may be gay, lesbian or bi-sexual, it is important for you to deal with your own emotions first. Although science has still not given us an answer to the question of what determines sexual orientation, it is misguided to think of yourself as the cause. It's much more probable that sexual orientation is just another card dealt in the big genetic poker game at birth.

The increasing openness of our society will make life much easier for your teen than for those in generations past. Still, your child will need your unconditional love and support more than ever. Dealing with sexual identity is hard enough for any teen, but it is that much harder for one who senses that he or she is going against the grain. Knowing that a parent values you as you are, no matter what, can make all the difference in the world.

Skills for Talking about Your Values

Show respect. Your teen is entitled to his own opinions. If he believes something you don't, avoid making disparaging or disapproving remarks. Keep the lines of communication open.

Avoid communication blocks. Otherwise, you may not only end the conversation with your teen; you may also motivate her to rebel against your values. If you command your teen to believe something, then the only way for her to feel as if she has power over herself is to believe the opposite!

Listen for feelings. Your teen's feelings change rapidly during these years. He may not know why he holds certain values. Help him to decide for himself by listening closely and repeating what you hear. For *example:*

"It sounds like you felt embarrassed when all the guys were talking about how far they got with their dates."

"So you're saying you think Dad and I make too big a deal out of drinking—that you believe it's just something teenagers do these days to have a good time."

Encourage your teen when he expresses a value you approve of. For example, if you would like your teenage son to learn to treat women respectfully, catch him being respectful and make a positive comment. For example:

"I couldn't help overhearing you talking with Mike in the kitchen tonight. I heard you say that it isn't cool to refer to a girl as 'easy'. I just wanted to tell you that I agree with you, and I'm proud of you for saying that to him."

Respect your teen's opinions, even if you disagree, and try to avoid judging or speaking to her harshly if she opens up.

Talk about values and beliefs, not just the facts. When you're discussing the touchy subjects of drugs, sex, and violence with your teen, keep in mind that she really needs to trust you before she'll confide in you about personal issues. Earn her trust by telling stories that reveal your own struggles to do the right thing—as long as you feel comfortable doing so and you think the story will benefit your teen. Also, respect your teen's opinions, even if you disagree, and try to avoid judging or speaking to her harshly if she opens up.

It seems like an unwritten rule that teens will adopt beliefs and values with which their parents disapprove. When this happens, remember that teens often try values the way they do styles of clothes: they change often; they are sometimes chosen

simply for shock value; they will probably be outgrown with time. By staying low-key and non-judgmental, you may one day find that you have been more of an influence than you thought at the time.

What happens if your beliefs differ dramatically from your teen's? Must you remain silent? Not at all! Instead, you can disagree with your teen respectfully, and calmly state your own opinion. This works best with palms up and an "I don't know what you'll decide" attitude. For example:

"I respect your right to think of sex as just another way for people to enjoy each other. My own opinion, however, is

Family Talks

Family talks focus on specific topics and values of importance to family members. Subjects can range from the "big three" of drugs, sexuality, and violence, to a wide range of topics: honesty, depression, television viewing, family roots, career choices, race relations, equality, advertising—anything about which family members have opinions and stories to share. It is up to you and your family to determine what topic you will discuss and how often. Although it's not advisable for parents to dictate values, you *can* teach and reinforce values by providing your teen with information and sound reasoning, as long as you always demonstrate these values through your actions. The following tips will help you plan and conduct a successful family talk.

1. Plan how you will introduce the topic.

This step applies to the first talk only, since family members will pick the topics together from then on. For example:

"The topic I'd like to introduce for this week's family talk is 'honesty.'"

2. Think of questions that will stimulate discussion.

For example:

- Why do you think it's important to be honest?
- How is keeping agreements a form of honesty?
- How do you feel when someone has lied to you or has not kept an agreement?
- There is an African proverb that goes: "One lie undoes 1000 truths." What does that mean to you?

3. Before having your talk, write down key points you want to make.

For example:

- The more people trust you, the more they can accept your word without having to check up on you.
- The more we trust you, the more freedom we can give you.
- When you need to change an agreement, talk to the other person and work out an alternative.
- We feel better about ourselves when we know are being honest.

4. Find support materials to help provide information or stimulate discussion.

Influencing your teen's values will require accurate information and sound reasoning. With topics such as drugs, sexuality, or violence you may want to do some research on your own to update your knowledge. Look for web pages from reliable sources, videos, excerpts from books, newspapers, and magazine articles. Watching certain television shows together can be a starting place for a family talk. Keep your eyes open, and you'll find many such resources for making your talks more interesting and informative.

5. Establish ground rules for your talks.

Using good communication skills can mean the difference between a positive family talk and a frustrating experience for everyone. Get agreement from the entire family on ground rules to help everyone communicate effectively. Use the following tips as a starting point.

Communication Tips	
DO	**DON'T**
Speak respectfully.	Put anyone's ideas down.
Invite everyone's ideas.	Interrupt.
Share how you think and feel.	Monopolize the discussion.
Try to see issues from other people's points of view.	Consider nobody's point of view except your own.
Compliment /encourage others.	Criticize others or call names.

If your teen violates one of these rules, simply remind him with a firm, calm comment. For example:

"We agreed that we wouldn't criticize each other, right?"

Once you establish ground rules for your family talks, it will be easier to keep everyone in a positive frame of mind.

that sex can be something very special, if it's saved for a special time with a special person. I'm sure that casual sex can be fun, but I think you pay a price for treating it cheaply. You may never know how really great it can be when it's used only as an expression of love and commitment."

The soft-sell approach by a father in the above example will give his son something to think about. The father has not forced a confrontation; rather, he has left the door open for his son to accept this view as his own. Dad's tone is caring rather than judgmental, and he has appealed to his son's sense of reason rather than using his authoritative position to command agreement.

Once you begin looking, you will find many opportunities to begin a discussion about values. Use TV shows, movies, and news items as openers. For example:

"I saw something on a TV movie last night that I wanted your opinion on. This guy and girl meet in a bar and get pretty drunk. They go home together and have sex, but they are either too drunk or just don't care because they don't use birth control. She gets pregnant. He says it's not his fault because he was drunk, and besides, it's the woman's job to take care of protection. What do you think?"

10 Prevention Strategies for Parents

Strategy #2. Educate your teens about the risks of drugs, sexuality, and violence.

Teens get a lot of information about drugs, sexuality and violence from other teens. Unfortunately, much of this "street" information is either inaccurate or one-sided because teens often emphasize the exciting aspects while downplaying or entirely ignoring the risks. To help balance this information bias, teens need to receive accurate and thorough information from other sources.

Many schools have programs to help inform teens about the real dangers involved with substance use, sexual behavior, and violence. If you are fortunate enough to have such a program in your teen's school, find out exactly what the program is teaching. Besides making sure that the program fits with your own value system, you will probably learn useful information that you can then reinforce in conversations with your teen.

Regardless of whether or not your teen learns about drugs, sexuality, and violence at school, it is important for you to be part of your teen's education on these subjects. Rather than having one long talk, it's more effective to have short but frequent discussions about these topics with your teen. This creates an open line of communication that can be extremely valuable as your teen meets challenging situations. As you engage your teen in these talks, keep the following points in mind:

- **Be prepared.** To be convincing, you need more than emotion. You need facts. Know the harmful effects of drugs, including nicotine, alcohol, and marijuana, which many teens mistakenly think are harmless. Know the risks involved in sexual activity and the facts about violence in your community. If your school has programs in any of these areas, get involved. At the very least, look at any available program materials so that you can use the information in discussions with your teen. You can get information through the resource list at the back of this book and from the more extensive resource guide at www.ActiveParenting.com/ParentingTeens.

- **Don't get hooked into an argument.** If you become overbearing or disrespectful during a discussion, you give your teen a reason to tune out or to rebel. So avoid getting drawn into an argument if you enter territory in which you and your teen disagree. And don't despair if your teen does not seem receptive to your information: Even teens who initially resist the facts may consider them later.

- **Invite your teen's input.** Ask for his view on the topic and express interest in hearing what information he can share. Keep the tone friendly. This is a discussion, not a lecture, so you shouldn't be the only one talking. Encourage your teen to speak openly by speaking openly yourself. If you decide that more information is needed about the topic, ask your teen for help in researching and gathering more information.

- **Come from caring, not authority.** You will influence your teen more by talking in terms of caring about her well-being than by dictating and demanding obedience. You can always say, "Do you have any idea how much I love you?" or "I care about your health and safety more than you can imagine."

Topics to Discuss with Your Teen

There are so many important topics that teens need to know about… How do you choose which ones to discuss? The following list can help you plan. Of course, your own values and what you know about your teen should influence the topics you choose to talk about, especially in the area of sexuality.

Tobacco, alcohol, and other drugs

- Specific drugs, their effects and risks (including nicotine, alcohol, and marijuana)

- The physical, psychological, and social effects of using any drug

- The consequences of breaking the law

- The increased chances of engaging in other risky behavior while under the influence of a drug (for example, having sex while under the influence of alcohol.)

Sexuality

- The reproductive process and birth control: Whether you believe in abstinence, natural family planning, or methods such as condoms or pills, it is important that your teen be aware of the risks and benefits of each. Don't assume they already know the facts!

- Sexually Transmitted Diseases (STDs). AIDS is still a big sexual risk facing teens today, yet most teens act as if they are immune. Teens should also know about herpes, syphilis, gonorrhea, chlamydia, venereal warts, and other STDs, as these are also very dangerous.

Violence

- Stranger danger: Which situations leave a teen vulnerable to rape, abduction, or other violence by a stranger? What can you and your teen do to reduce these risks?

- Fighting: How do conflicts grow into fights? What are the risks? What could your teen do instead of fighting? If your teen is on the sidelines of a fight, how should he react?

- Date violence: Fifteen percent of teenage girls report that an acquaintance tried to force sex with them. Forty percent report knowing someone who has been hit or beaten by a boyfriend. Discuss with your sons and daughters why boys hurt girls. Emphasize that using physical force or emotional manipulation to get someone to have sex is wrong. Discuss the value of self-esteem and mutual respect with regard to sexuality.

On the next page you'll see a list of topics that represent risk factors in teens' lives. Use this list to choose a topic to discuss with your teen, or use it to generate ideas about other possible discussion topics. Whichever topic you choose to discuss, use articles, books, and videos to help you present the information with knowledgeable authority. For instance, you and your teen could watch a video or read an article together or separately, then talk about it afterwards.

The following dialogue is an example of how a talk about AIDS and other sexually transmitted diseases might go between a parent and a teen:

Father: You've probably heard a lot about sexually transmitted diseases (STDs). I thought we should talk about it ourselves. What do you know about them?

Son: Dad, they teach us about this stuff at school.

Father: Well, there are a lot of things that *I* want to talk to you about. This is just one of them.

Son: Oh, well, I know they are called STDs because you can get them from having sex. I know that syphilis and gonorrhea are two of them...oh, yeah and AIDS.

Father: Right, and Herpes, Chlamydia, HPV, and lots of other stuff.

Son: Wow, that's a lot of nasty stuff.

Father: You are right about that.

Son: But they can cure them all, right?

Father: Well, they can cure most of them, if they catch it in time. But not all of them. How much do you know about AIDS?

Son: AIDS is a disease that can kill you. That it has to do with the immune system. And that you can get it from having sex with a gay guy.

Father: Well, that's partially right. It is a disease that affects the body's immune system. In fact, "AIDS" actually stands for Acquired Immune Deficiency Syndrome. In other words, it attacks the body's immune system, leaving the person helpless to fight off diseases. People who get AIDS may eventually die from some other disease, because their bodies can't fight it off.

Son: Yeah, I remember now, it sort of takes away their defenses.

Father: Exactly. And you're also right about it being sexually transmitted. Because the AIDS virus is carried in blood and in semen, most people who get AIDS get it from sexual intercourse. But some people have also gotten AIDS from blood transfusions, although this is more rare because people are testing blood better than they used to. Also, drug users can get it from sharing needles.But there is one thing that you're a little bit off on.

Son: What's that?

Father: People don't get AIDS only from gays. In fact, the AIDS virus doesn't know a gay person from a straight person from a bisexual person. All it knows is it can be transmitted through blood and semen, which means that it can also be carried through regular heterosexual intercourse.

Son: Well, at least they can cure it now.

Father: Not so fast. They have made a lot of progress in treating AIDS, and there are treatments now that let people live a lot longer. But there is still no cure.

Son: Well, how can you keep from getting it? Is there a vaccine?

Father: No, not yet. The only sure way to keep from getting AIDS is not to have sex.

Son: I'm supposed to never have sex?!

Father: Well it doesn't have to be quite that drastic. If you wait until you get married, and you're sure that your partner doesn't have AIDS, and if the two of you are faithful during your marriage, then you can be 100% sure that you can be as sexual as you want to be and not get AIDS.

Son: Can't you use a condom or something like that?

Father: Probably. If you use them correctly, they're supposed to prevent AIDS in most cases. But they're not 100% safe.

Son: Well, if I ever had sex before getting married, I think I'd use one.

Father: Well, I hope you decide to wait until you're married. But if you don't, I'm real glad to hear you say that. In fact, I'd say that anybody who has sex these days without a condom is risking their lives. I came across a web site that I think you'll find interesting. It's got some good information about AIDS and other sexually transmitted diseases. I'll e-mail you the link, and then I'd like to hear your opinion about it.

10 Prevention Strategies for Parents

Strategy #3. Filter OUT the negative and IN the positive influences.

Just as governments try to filter out illegal drugs before they get into the system and reach their citizens, Active parents act as filters to prevent harmful events from influencing their teens.

We've learned about the need to instill qualities of character in teens so that they will be able to make good decisions by themselves when challenged to do so. We've learned about moving teens into success cycles so that they can use their best thinking, feeling, and doing to meet such challenges. And we've learned about the importance of allowing teens to learn from the natural consequences of their actions.

Even so, there are still times when parents should GET IN THE WAY! The technical term for this is *interdiction*, and it's no accident that this term is often applied to the drug trade, as in "drug enforcement agents *interdicted* illegal drugs coming into the country." Just as governments try to filter out illegal drugs before they get into the system and reach their citizens, Active parents act as filters to prevent harmful events from influencing their teens.

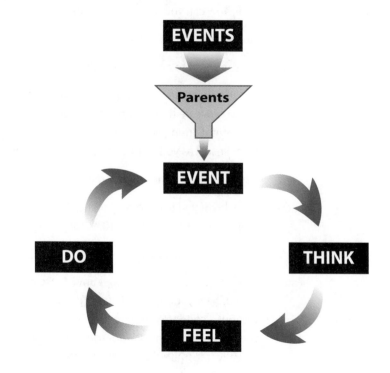

As the diagram shows, parents can sometimes come between an event and their teen, filtering out the event's ability to influence the teen's Think-Feel-Do Cycle. The goal is not to censor every negative influence that your teen might experience, but to limit them while at the same time helping your teen put them into the proper perspective. Parents should aim to filter out events that are excessively dangerous in themselves or likely to promote beliefs and values that are harmful—particularly events that might encourage the use of tobacco, alcohol or other drugs, reckless sexuality, and violence.

The goal is not to censor every negative influence that your teen might experience, but to limit them while at the same time helping your teen put them into the proper perspective.

Ways to Filter OUT Negative Influences

- Become familiar with the media your teen uses—and agree on reasonable usage guidelines.

- Use rating systems and parental controls to help regulate media.

- Watch some of what your teen watches, and then discuss the messages presented.

- Learn to use parental controls and usage trackers provided by Internet providers and other methods of monitoring what your teen is accessing online.

- If practical, keep computers in public areas of the home where you can easily check to make sure only sites that you approve are being opened.

- Talk with the parents of your teen's friends and encourage them to be vigilant also. Teens will often seek out homes where the restrictions are lax, so support each other.

- Set and enforce reasonable curfews.

- Know where your teen is and have him check in periodically.

- Get to know the teens and adults your teen spends time with. Talk with her about choosing friends and how friends influence each other.

- Subtly influence who your teen spends time with.

The reason you want to be "subtle" about who your teen spends time with is that teens are very sensitive about who they choose for friends. If you come on too strong, they may rebel and sneak together just to prove to themselves that they have control. The exception is if your teen's friend is breaking the law. Then you have to risk the backlash and let your teen know that this friend (or group of friends) is off limits—at least until they get their act together. Here are a few subtle ways to influence who your teen hangs out with:

- Try to choose a neighborhood and school where other families are likely to share your values.

- Encourage your teen to join teams or participate in activities that will promote positive interaction.

- Talk together non-judgmentally about what makes for good friends.

Keep in mind that friends will play an important role in your teen's life, and the quality of those friends could make a significant difference in the decisions your teen makes.

Parents as Filters: Your Teen Online

Media and technology—and particularly the Internet—account for much of what influences today's teens. Teens are more "plugged in" than ever before. Their ways of communicating, socializing, and meeting new people are dramatically different from what you knew when you were teens, even if it wasn't that long ago. A great deal of social interaction among teens takes place via the Internet, often through social networking sites.

Teens like these sites because they connect them to the world. They provide a place where teens can create and showcase who they are and keep up with their friends. But most of all, teens love it because it's *their place*. In fact, one of the reasons these sites are so popular with teens is precisely because parents often don't "get it."

It can be a real challenge for parents to find the right approach to the technology that has become so much a part of teens' lives. One parent said, "When I reveal that I don't know how to use the latest protocol in instant messaging, my kids think I'm hopelessly old fashioned. But when I try to chat with them through their personal web sites, it's an invasion of privacy."

Regardless of how your teen accepts your presence in their plugged-in world, you need to be aware of the risks involved and how you might help to filter them out of your teen's life.

- ■ **Age limits on social networking sites can't be enforced.** Many social networking sites are intended for adults, and they contain topics, media, and links to content that are not appropriate for teens and pre-teens. Although these sites often have some type of security in place to keep minors from entering or becoming members, it's not enough. Teens can and will gain access. Try to be sure that the social networking sites where your teen is a member are specifically for youths.

- ■ **Teens often give out too much personal information and communicate with strangers**. Everyone has heard horror stories about online predators who pretend to be teens in order to lure real teens to meet with them face to face. Your teens need to know that these stories are not made up. Emphasize to them the importance of not revealing personal information to anyone who they only know from online interactions. Ask your teen you tell you immediately if any online friends ask to meet in person or if she has been drawn into any conversation that made her feel uncomfortable.

- ■ **Teens may post inappropriate content that can have serious consequences**. Teens may not realize that what they put online is often freely searchable by anyone who wants to find it. That includes teachers, employers, grandparents, siblings, and of course, parents. It may even include law enforcement, depending on the content. To a 16-year-old teen, posting a revealing video online might seem like a great way to tell the world who he is, but it will seem like an incredibly stupid mistake when, two years later, a college admissions officer uses a passed-along version of the video as a reason to reject his application.

- **Anonymity can lead teens to act disrespectfully or with fewer inhibitions.** People behave differently in the anonymous world of online communication. They may assume an entirely new identity, or they may just be a bolder version of themselves. Parents should help teens understand that just because their true identities may not be known by people they are communicating with online, it does not mean it's OK to insult others or to abandon their sense of right and wrong. Teens may also invent online identities that claim far more sexual experience and who are more willing to take more risks than they are in real life. Teens might view this as harmless fun, but encountering the wrong person with this false identity could lead them into dangerous territory.

- **Online relationships may be based on false information.** Just as your teen may assume a false identity online, he needs to be aware that everyone he meets online may not be who or what they claim to be. Encourage your teen never to make decisions based on the claims of online acquaintances—especially not to reveal any personal information or to give them money or other items without communicating through a secure and well-established exchange system such as eBay (and even then, they need to be careful).

- **Misinformation is rampant, especially about drugs and sexuality.** People say you can find anything on the Internet, and it's true that if you conduct a search on virtually any subject, you will find that someone, somewhere has posted information about it. Most adults know that much of this information is many steps removed from its original source and is often more opinion than fact, therefore it's not trustworthy. Teens may need to be reminded of this. Chances are, they're searching online for information about topics that they are afraid or embarrassed to ask parents about. They need to know that much of what they find may not be accurate. You can help by providing your teen with a list of trusted web sites that address topics such as sexuality and the harmful effects of alcohol, tobacco, and other drugs. And you can help your teen by making sure she knows you're there to answer questions without judging her.

Filtering IN Positive Events

If you can filter *out* certain negative events that might harm or negatively influence your teen, you can also filter *in*, or encourage, positive events that can help build character and lead to a success cycle. As much as you might like to think otherwise, no teen gets everything he needs from his parents. They need to supplement what parents give them with input from other adults and peers. You can help this process along by thinking of creative ways to provide encouraging influences on your teen's development. For example:

Positive adult influences: Make sure that your teen has positive contact with other adult mentors, such as:

- Spiritual youth group leaders

- Sports coaches

- Teachers

- Adult friends

- Relatives

- Mentors in programs such as Big Brother/Big Sister

Media: There are many positive role models and lessons in books, movies, music, TV and the Internet. Help your teen find and take advantage of this positive input and you will strengthen many positive values.

Summer camp and other away-from-home programs: A great variety of camps and programs are available for teens during summer vacation: not only traditional summer camps, but also specialized camps where teens can focus on particular talents or areas of interest such as music, sports, or wildlife observation. Or teens may prefer programs in which they can take unique classes, go on a spiritual retreat, or complete a volunteer project. The opportunities are diverse and can be rewarding to teens in many different ways—especially as a way to experience a little independence. Counselors, teachers, and other staff can be a wonderful influence on teen development. Although, to be fair, I am particularly biased in favor of a camp experience having grown up as the son of a camp director. I always valued the lessons I learned from many of my own counselors, and have heard hundreds of adults, even one national leader, thank my father for the positive effect he had on their lives.

A loving spiritual education: When delivered in a loving and supportive manner, a spiritual education will provide many positive lessons of character as well as faith.

A good academic environment: Let's face it—all schools are not created equal. Your teen will spend more time at school than any other place other than bed, so find the best one that your financial situation will allow, even if it means moving. The value of a good educational environment is more than just the teachers and facilities. Just as important is the quality of the other kids and families that your teen goes to school and hangs out with, as they will also be an influence.

Positive peers: The term *peer pressure* has a bad reputation, but the fact is that peer pressure can be either positive OR negative. Help get your teen involved with a group of positive peers—ones who reject tobacco, alcohol and other drugs, reckless sexuality, and violence—and their positive influence with make it easier for both your teen and you. Of course, just as you should be subtle in discouraging negative friends, you need to be subtle in encouraging positive ones. Getting your teen involved in healthy activities is a good way to start.

10 Prevention Strategies for Parents

Strategy #4. Establish clear guidelines for behavior.

I've emphasized the importance of opening communication with your teen by taking a non-judgmental attitude about whatever she thinks or feels. The same is NOT true for behavior. You want to be clear that some behaviors are off limits. Taking the time to agree on clear guidelines for behavior with your teen can pay off greatly when your teen has to make a choice. It is like taking a test and knowing the correct answers ahead of time. A problem-prevention talk (as you learned about in Chapter 4) is an ideal way to proceed.

Let's review the five steps of the problem-prevention talk:

1. Identify a potential problems or risk.

2. Share your thoughts and feelings about the problem and acknowledge your teen's thoughts and feelings.

3. Generate guidelines through brainstorming and negotiation (within limits that you can live with).

4. Decide on logical consequences for violating the guidelines (if necessary).

5. Follow up to ensure that guidelines were followed and to enforce consequences (if necessary).

Not every situation in a teen's life calls for parents to impose guidelines around it. In fact, it's easy to go too far and end up overprotecting your teen with so many guidelines that she has no decisions left to make for herself. As we discussed earlier in this chapter, parents who overprotect their teen fail to prepare her for future independence. So choose carefully where you establish guidelines. The best place to start is with situations in your teen's life that may introduce risks related to drugs, sexuality, and violence. For example:

- curfews

- having friends over, or spending nights out

- going to parties

- when and how to use physical force as defense

- going places that could be dangerous

- dating

- driving, or riding with friends

Establishing a "No-Use" Rule

One of the few hard and fast guidelines for behavior that I recommend is a "no-use" rule: Parents and teens make an agreement (either verbally or in writing) stating that everyone in the family will obey the law as it applies to the use of tobacco, alcohol, and other drugs. It can be stated like this:

> *"No use of illegal drugs by anyone in the family, and no use of alcohol or nicotine by anyone under the legal age of ___ ."*

The no-use rule can be part of your family's discussion about the harmful effects of alcohol and other drugs. All members of the family who are old enough to understand it should sign.

Be careful not to sabotage your own rule by giving the message that "all kids will try it" or that "rules were made to be broken."

Once the rule is established, it is important for you to let your teen know that you expect her to abide by the rule. This means no experimenting or social use, either. Be careful not to sabotage your own rule by giving the message that "all kids will try it" or that "rules were made to be broken."

If you want your teen to satisfy his curiosity about what alcohol is like, it may be legal for you to allow the use of this substance in your own home. Many states in the U.S. have this exception to their laws; check to be sure that your own state is among them. Then, if you choose to provide this supervised opportunity for your teen to try alcohol, I strongly recommend that you make it a one-time event and DO NOT ALLOW REGULAR USE. There is growing evidence that alcohol can interfere with normal teenage development. Of course, marijuana and other illegal substances should not be used by anyone, even to satisfy one's curiosity about what they're like. The risk of harm or addiction is too great. Likewise, parents should not allow their teens to try tobacco even once. Many habitual users—both smokers and those who use chewing tobacco—report getting a "buzz" after their first try. The best choice is to make "No tobacco—not now, not ever" your policy with your teens on this deadly substance.

For rules to carry impact, you must back them up with consequences. If you have no reason to suspect your teen of breaking the no-use rule, discuss consequences with her in general terms only. You might say something like:

"Let's be clear about something. For us to continue to feel good about giving you more freedom and more responsibility, we have to be able to trust you. This no-use rule is largely a matter of trust. We won't be there looking over your shoulder every minute. We won't lock you in your room during your free time. But if you should break that trust, then the responsible thing for us to do is to keep a closer eye on you. That means keeping you home more often, checking up on you more regularly, and otherwise cutting back on your freedom. And since using alcohol or other drugs when driving can be deadly, we would want to protect you and others by not allowing you to use the car."

If your teen has a history of drug or alcohol use, or if she breaks the no-use rule, then you can use more specific consequences. Rather than relying on the common and usually ineffectual consequence of grounding, it will have more impact if you suspend specific privileges, possessions, and favors that your teen wants from you. Remember, it's important that these consequences are logically related to the breaking of the no-use rule. The loss of driving privileges is logically connected to the use of mind-altering substances because they make driving unsafe. Not being allowed to go to parties or concerts for a period of time is logical because trust is needed in these situations, and your teen has temporarily lost your trust. By talking with your teen, your spouse, and other adults, you can come up with a list of consequences that will be meaningful to your teen.

After your teen has experienced the consequences for breaking a no-use rule, it's important for you to specify how your teen can earn back your trust.

After your teen has experienced the consequences for breaking a no-use rule, it's important for you to specify how your teen can earn back your trust. If she feels she can never win it back, or that her freedom is gone forever, she may rebel and do what she wants to do anyway.

Family Meeting: Preventing High-Risk Behavior

The Problem-Prevention Talk is a model that will serve parents well in many scenarios. For this chapter's family meeting, you'll have another opportunity to practice this useful five-step process. This time, have a Problem-Prevention Talk to follow Prevention Strategy #3: Establish guidelines for behavior. The guide sheets on pages 193-194 will take you step-by-step through the process.

For step 1, you will need to choose a situation in your teen's life that would benefit from guidelines—that is, a situation in which guidelines will serve to prevent real risk. Try to avoid any tendency to overprotect your teen by setting unnecessary guidelines. The list on page 187 may help you choose an appropriate situation.

By the meeting's end, you will have established behavior guidelines for the area you chose to address. And, if necessary, you will have decided on a logical consequence in case your teen violates the guidelines.

Family Enrichment Activity: Expressing Love

Building a positive relationship with your teen is an ongoing process, and it takes steady effort. It includes having fun together, teaching specific skills, and showing respect. Most of all, a positive relationship between parent and teen needs love. All

teens need to know that whatever else may happen, their parents love them. You can show your teen you love him in many small ways: a kiss, a pat on the back, tousling his hair, putting your arm around his shoulder. But you also need to *tell* him that you love him. The words may be awkward if you're not used to saying them. But they're beautiful to your teen, even if he rolls his eyes in embarrassment.

Your assignment for this family enrichment activity is to find ways to express your love to your teen, including actually saying "I love you." The guide sheet on page 195 will help you.

chapter **5**

Home Activities

1. Complete the "Parents as Role Models" questionnaire on page 192.

2. Have a Problem-Prevention Talk with your teen about a high-risk behavior, using the five-step process you learned in Session 4. Then complete the guide sheets on page 193-194.

3. Express love to your teen every day, and fill out the guide sheet on page 195.

Parent Role-Model Questionnaire

There are no right or wrong answers to the following questions. They are designed to help you be aware of your habits and behavior with regard to sexuality, violence, and the use of alcohol, tobacco, and other drugs. As you reflect on your responses, ask yourself what messages you may be sending to your teens through these actions and if what you do matches the values you wish to teach your teens.

1. Do you drink alcohol? _____ How many drinks do you have per week? _____

2. Do you use alcohol or other drugs to comfort yourself when you're depressed? _____

3. Have your children ever seen you drunk or high on another drug? _____

4. Do you seek out social functions where there is a lot of drinking? _____
   Do you avoid ones where there is little or no drinking? _____

5. In your home, do people joke and tell stories about getting drunk or high and doing crazy things? _____

6. Do your children ever hear you and your spouse arguing about one of you having had too much to drink? _____

7. Do you smoke cigarettes? _____ How many a day? _____

8. Have you ever warned your children about smoking while you were smoking? _____
   How about drinking? _____

9. Do you drive while under the influence of alcohol or other mood-altering drugs? _____

10. Have you had sexual partners (other than a long-term partner or spouse) stay overnight while your children were home? _____ How often? _____

11. When you're angry, do you:
    Shout? _____ Use curse words? _____ Insult others? _____ Throw or break things? _____

12. Have you ever physically hurt anyone out of anger? _____ Are your children aware of it? _____

Problem-Prevention Talk: Preventing High-Risk Behavior

Follow the five steps of the Problem-Prevention Talk model to establish guidelines for your teen's behavior in a high-risk situation of your choosing.

Step 1: Identify a potential problem and/or risk.

At this meeting, we are establishing guidelines for the following situation: _____

_____

Step 2: Share your thoughts and feelings about this problem, and acknowledge your teen's thoughts and feelings.

My thoughts and feelings: _____

_____

My teen's thoughts and feelings: _____

_____

Step 3: Generate guidelines through brainstorming and negotiation (within limits that you can live with).

Brainstorming Space

Continued on next page...

GUIDELINES:

_____

_____

_____

Step 4: Decide on logical consequences for violating the guidelines (if necessary).

If the guidelines are violated, the consequences will be: _____

_____

_____

Step 5: Follow up to ensure that guidelines were followed and to enforce consequences (if necessary).

Were guidelines followed? _____

Were consequences enforced? _____

What did you like about your Problem Prevention Talk? _____

_____

What will you do differently next time? _____

_____

What topics would you like to have future Problem Prevention Talks about? _____

_____

Family Enrichment Activity: Expressing Love

Remember when...

Recall a time when you were a teen and an adult in your life expressed love to you. Maybe it was a parent, a grandparent, another relative, or a teacher. Maybe the expression was through words, maybe through an action like a pat on the back or a hug.

Describe the experience: _____

_____

_____

How did it make you feel? _____

_____

_____

Expressing Love at Home

To help you remember to tell your teen you love him or her, fill in this chart:

Teen's Name	Your Expression	Your Teen's Response

Drugs, Sexuality, and Violence: Reducing the Risks

Part 2

A middle-aged man stares blankly at the images appearing on his video monitor late into the night while his wife and children sleep. He has told himself over and over that he must stop, that it just isn't worth the risk to his marriage, his family, his job. Yet he finds his fingers at the keyboard automatically taking him back to the familiar haunts of cyber space whenever he has the opportunity—sometimes all night, if he's sure that his wife is sound asleep. He tells himself that this is the last time, but he knows it isn't. The urge is too powerful. Like millions of other Americans, he is addicted to pornography.

▲ ▲ ▲

A middle-aged woman sips another glass of wine and laughs. She is feeling warm and happy as the alcohol finds its way into her bloodstream and races upwards into her welcoming brain. She knows she drinks too much. Her doctors have warned her of the consequences, but so what? It's my life and if a little wine (okay, a lot of wine) helps me get through, so be it. That's what her father always said. Feeling a pang of sadness at this memory, she tips her glass and drains it. Her father had died of "alcohol related causes" in his fifties, which she knows she should take as a clear warning to stop. But not tonight. Tonight she feels too good to stop. Like millions of other Americans, she is addicted to alcohol.

Unless you have ever experienced the powerlessness of addiction yourself, you may be thinking that the people in these two stories simply lack the will to give up some bad habits. If you *have* experienced the horrors of addiction in your own life, or even if you've seen it close up in a parent or sibling, you know the difference between a bad habit and an addiction, and you would do anything in your power to keep your children from going down that same lonely path.

Here is some of what we know about addiction:

- Addiction can occur whether the chemicals that fuel the addiction are introduced from the outside (as with tobacco, alcohol, and other drugs) or produced inside the brain itself (as with sex, gambling, work, and perhaps even forms of anger and violence).

- Some addictions are stronger than others. For example, a coffee (or caffeine) addiction is mild compared to an addiction to cocaine.

- Most people are not "general addicts". Addiction to one thing does not imply that a person has a general tendency to develop addictions. For example, a person who could easily become addicted to pornography is not necessarily at risk for becoming addicted to alcohol.

- Addictive tendencies are genetically passed down through families. For example, a teen whose mother is an alcoholic is eight times more likely to become addicted to alcohol himself.

- The length of time it takes to become fully addicted varies from substance to substance and from person to person. Alcohol addiction may take three years to become full blown while crack cocaine can addict some people in a single use.

- Addictive behavior—drinking alcohol, smoking cigarettes, gambling, viewing pornography—often begins as a way to relieve stress and alter one's mood. Many addicts say that their addiction began in adolescence for just this reason.

- The consequences of addictions usually follow this simple pattern:

  Phase 1.   *Pleasure*

  Phase 2.   *Pleasure + problems*

  Phase 3.   *Problems*

Scientists are learning more and more about the physiology of addiction and may be able to cure it in the future. But for now, our best bet is to help teens understand the risks and make smart choices that will keep them from having to cope with addiction down the road.

Drugs, Sexuality, and Violence: More Prevention Strategies

Of course, addiction is not the only risk of misusing drugs, sexuality, or violence. Health, safety, good judgment, success, and your teen's life itself are also at risk. In Chapter 5, we covered four of the ten prevention strategies for reducing your teen's risk of involvement with drugs, sexuality, or violence:

Strategy #1.   **Be a positive role model and teacher of values.**

Strategy #2.   **Educate your teen about the risks.**

Strategy #3.   **Filter <u>out</u> negative influences and <u>in</u> positive ones.**

Strategy #4.   **Establish clear guidelines for behavior.**

In this chapter we will look at the remaining five:

Strategy #5.   **Monitor and supervise teen behavior.**

Strategy #6.   **Work with other parents.**

Strategy #7.   **Provide healthy opportunities for challenge.**

Strategy #8.   **Consult with your teen about how to resist peer pressure.**

Strategy #9.   **Identify and confront high-risk behavior.**

Strategy #10. **Calmly manage a crisis should one occur.**

10 Prevention Strategies for Parents

Strategy #5. Monitor and supervise teen behavior.

I heard a tragic story about a fight that broke out between teens from two rival high schools at a party. There had been a lot of beer drinking, and passions—as well as tensions—were high. During the fight, one of the teens pulled a knife and stabbed another, who died on the way to the hospital. This was not in a rough neighborhood or an inner-city setting. It took place in an affluent suburb of a typical American city.

You may expect that the parents of the house were out of town, as is often the case with teen parties. They were not. In fact, they were upstairs watching TV. When asked why they were not downstairs supervising the party, they answered, *Because we didn't want to get in the way.*

Their response is not that unusual. The irony, however, is that it is part of a parent's job to get in the way. Parents must be willing and able to provide safe limits on their teens' freedom until the teens become capable of establishing these limits on their own. Research clearly shows that positive parental involvement is a key factor in preventing delinquency, drug use, school failure, pregnancy, crime, and a host of other teen problems. Here are some guidelines:

Research clearly shows that positive parental involvement is a key factor in preventing delinquency, drug use, school failure, pregnancy, crime, and a host of other teen problems.

Provide things for your teen to do. Although it is unwise to try to monitor every moment of your teenager's day, it's worse to allow him to have a great deal of unsupervised time, which would put him at a much higher risk for drifting into negative peer groups and developing problems. Suggest healthy and challenging activities for your teen to do both alone and with other teens. Encourage him to take on a hobby that will provide something for him to do during otherwise idle time. As he demonstrates responsibility in handling unstructured time, you can gradually relax your supervision and influence.

Know where your teen is and who she's with. Make a habit of asking your teen to tell you her plans before she goes out. Be sure that she knows how to contact you or another responsible adult if she needs to. Establish a check-in rule that you both can live with. If they could get away with it, some parents would have their teens call them every 15 minutes to report their whereabouts. However, teens would view such a requirement as mistrust. But asking for an occasional check-in call is reasonable and responsible. Even in families in which both parents work outside the home, telephone check-ins can help parents monitor behavior.

Set and enforce curfews. This should be agreed upon by both you and your teen. Sit down with your teen and have a Problem-Prevention Talk to set guidelines, continuing your discussion until you have agreed on weekend and weekday curfews and consequences for missing them. Setting curfews is a good way to reduce later conflicts and misunderstandings. Be awake when your teen comes home to make sure she is following the guidelines. If she does a good job of keeping to the agreed-upon limits, her responsibilities should earn her greater freedom. Likewise, if the guidelines are violated, then logical consequences can be used to reduce freedom.

10 Prevention Strategies for Parents

Strategy #6. Work with other parents.

Napoleon Bonaparte observed that, "People do not want liberty; they want equality." This is particularly true of teens.

Teens have a tremendous support group—their peers—to back up their behavior. They instinctively understand the principle of power in numbers. Parents can also utilize this principle by forming parent support groups in their community. These "parent networks," as they are often called, can help parents agree on certain issues such as chaperoning, curfews, the need for regular communication among parents, and the unacceptability of teens using alcohol and other drugs.

Napoleon Bonaparte observed that, "People do not want liberty; they want equality." This is particularly true of teens. Parents know an uphill battle is coming when they hear the age-old retort, "But everyone else is …" How much easier it is for a teen to give up something he wants when his peers aren't being allowed to do it either!

If your teen's school does not already have a parent network, use an Active Parenting group to begin one. Talk to your school counselor, psychologist, or social worker about how you can get a group going. Use the Internet and other resources to connect, inform, and share your experience with other concerned parents. In this age of rapidly expanding communications technology, there are countless ways to network and support each other. Take advantage.

10 Prevention Strategies for Parents

Strategy #7. Provide healthy opportunities for challenge.

When I was seventeen, I had the opportunity to experience a month-long "Outward Bound" course in the Blue Ridge Mountains. Every morning at daybreak, we were roused from our sleep to run three miles to a mountain stream where we were doused in ice-cold water. The day only got harder after that: We ran, hiked, climbed, and otherwise pitted ourselves against the elements. It was the most physically demanding experience of my life, but when it was over, I felt that I had really achieved something. For one, I had moved from teenhood to adulthood.

The other four goals of behavior— belonging, power, protection, and withdrawal—are common to all young people, but challenge only emerges as a goal in the teen years.

Challenge is a basic goal of behavior for teens. The other four goals of behavior that we learned about in Chapter 4—belonging, power, protection, and withdrawal—are common to all young people, but challenge only emerges as a goal in the teen years. The need to be challenged is a powerful drive, and yet many teens do not get enough opportunities to do so in positive ways. For too many teens, life is boring. So they resort to challenging themselves through the negative approach of *thrill seeking* just to feel a rush of adrenaline and a sense of adventure. Drugs, sex, and violence offer easy but dangerous ways to accomplish this goal.

How can parents help? First, start working with your community leaders to make challenging activities available to all teens in your area. In the meantime, help your own teen to take advantage of activities that are already available. If it's a physical challenge your teen wants, look into adreneline-pumping activities like rock-climbing, mountain biking, or white-water rafting. Help your teen get involved with scouting or outdoor adventure programs such as Outward Bound. Organized sports offer excellent opportunities for healthy challenge, as well. School leagues, recreation department leagues, and youth groups such as the YMCA and Boys and Girls Clubs, offer plenty of opportunities for girls and boys to get physical in healthy ways.

In addition to physical challenges, you can also encourage your teen to pursue challenges of a more intellectual kind: hobbies and other interests in which they challenge themselves to develop skills and knowledge. Possibilities include debate groups, chess clubs, working on the school newspaper, skill-building jobs, junior business clubs, community service work, dance groups, and playing a musical instrument. If your teen can find an interest that challenges her to stick with it and do her best, her confidence will grow and she will satisfy her desire for excitement in positive ways.

10 Prevention Strategies for Parents

Strategy #8. Consult with teens about how to resist peer pressure.

Most people realize that to "just say no" to drugs, sexual activity, or violence is a lot easier said than done. Have you never knuckled under to people around you and eaten something that wasn't on your diet, or bought something you didn't really want? The pressure on teens, with their strong desire to belong, is a lot greater.

Peer pressure is more subtle and strong than most people realize. Imagine that four teens are sitting around talking, and one lights up a marijuana joint. Two of the others say, "Great!" and take a hit. The third hands it to your teen, expecting that she'll want to smoke some, too. Let's say she doesn't want to, but she doesn't want to look scared or inexperienced, either. She feels the pressure to do what they're doing without anyone actually telling her to follow along. What's she going to do? Say "no"? Go along with it anyway? Take a puff but not inhale? You can increase the chances of her saying "no" by coaching her ahead of time about how to handle such difficult situations in ways that don't make her feel foolish.

Resisting peer pressure requires three main things:

1. Knowing your rights

2. The courage to do what's right

3. A good comeback line

Let's go over these one by one.

1. Knowing your rights

Help your teen realize that she has the right to say "no" to peer pressure. Her goals and values for her life are important. She needs to know this. Also, encourage her by accepting that she may not always agree with you any more than she does her friends. You may feel frustrated when she argues with you, but she'll need that strong will to stand up to her peers when they want her to cave in.

2. The courage to do what's right

Help your teen recognize that he is strong enough to do what's right. Point out his strength each time he exhibits it.

Examples:

> *"I really appreciate you going to the wedding with us even though it meant not going to the game."*

> *"I'm proud of the way you told us the truth about the party this weekend, even though you knew we wouldn't let you go since it isn't supervised."*

3. A good comeback line

Because teens are desperate to save face in all circumstances, they need to be able to say "no" in a way that doesn't leave them feeling foolish. Give your teen some practice by going over potential peer pressure situations before they happen and helping your teen come up with comeback lines.

Situation #1:

"What's the matter, you're too chicken to fight?"

What could you say to your teen about violence or fighting?

_____

_____

What is a good comeback line you could suggest?

_____

_____

Here's a sample conversation between parent and teen:

Parent: *Okay, here's the situation. You pull into a parking lot just as another car is pulling in. You get the parking place, but the other guy gets out of the car and is really mad. You two start exchanging words, and you can see that he wants to fight. What do you do?*

Teen: *That's a hard one.*

Parent: *You're right. It is.*

Teen: *I'd tell him that we better cool down before the cops throw us both in jail.*

Parent: *Hey, that's pretty quick. Any other ideas?*

Situation #2:

"Here, take a hit off this joint."

What could you say to your teen about drugs?

_____

_____

What's a good comeback line you could suggest?

_____

_____

Here's a sample conversation between parent and teen:

Parent: *So what could you say if you were at a party and three guys just took a hit of marijuana and offered you a smoke?*

Teen: *No thanks?*

Parent: *Well, that would work. But what if they pushed harder?*

Teen: *I don't know.*

Parent: *Well, how about, "Are you crazy?! My parents will find out and I'll have to wait till I move out before I'm allowed to go to another party."*

Teen: *That's good. Or I could say, "You guys are idiots for putting that stuff in your body."*

Parent: *That would take a lot of courage. But it may make them think twice about what they're doing.*

Situation #3:

"Come on. Everybody's having sex these days!"

What could say to your teen about sex?

_____

_____

What's a good comeback line you could suggest:

_____

_____

Here's a sample conversation between parent and teen:

Parent: *What would you say if a girl got you alone and started undressing you?*

Teen: *Thank you, God?*

Parent: *That's not exactly the answer I was hoping for.*

Teen: *I'm kidding. That's not going to happen.*

Parent: *Don't be so sure. I read this true story in a magazine. A girl had been drinking and went into a boy's dorm room—they were in college. She came on to him and he slept with her. The next week she claimed rape, saying she was too drunk to know what she was doing. He didn't get convicted of rape, but he wound up having to leave school because everybody thought it was his fault.*

Teen: *Wow. That's not fair.*

Parent: *Maybe not, but what would you do if it happened to you?*

Teen: *I guess I'd tell her I'd better take her home so she can get some sleep.*

Parent: *That would take some willpower, but it's the right thing to do.*

Bullying Is Violence

One of the changes we have seen in the world since the last edition of this program is the recognition that bullying is a significant form of violence, one that often leads to much more serious expressions of violence. The news over this period has been rife with examples of bullying victims turned into suicide or homicide victims. We've also watched in horror as onetime victims of bullying suddenly snapped and sought revenge on others, often on innocent students, in some of the worst school shootings in history. What doesn't make the headlines are the personal stories of thousands of teens on whom bullying leaves its mark every day, diminishing both the bully and the victim. Fortunately, with awareness of bullying on the rise, schools are much more proactive than they once were, and programs designed to prevent bullying are becoming more common. Active parents can help, as well.

What is bullying?

- *Physical bullying:* hitting, kicking, pushing, choking, punching
- *Verbal bullying*: threatening, taunting, teasing, starting rumors, hate speech
- *Exclusion:* Excluding teens from group activities with the intention of making them feel bad. "You weren't invited to our party!" "No one wants to hang out with him;" "Don't be her friend."
- *Internet bullying:* Using the Internet to attack a victim verbally, often with lies and rumors, often anonymously.

What can parents do to prevent their own kids from bullying?

- Use an Active style of parenting (research shows that children raised under dictator and doormat styles are more often associated with bullying behavior.)
- Have a family meeting about bullying. Describe the different types of bullying. Explain why all of them are wrong and that bullying is unacceptable by anyone in your family.
- Find out the school's policy on bullying, and use that information to reinforce your arguments.
- Make it clear to your teen that logical consequences will follow if he engages in any kind of bullying behavior.
- If your teen gets involved in bullying, follow through with the consequences, but also ask questions like:

> What did you do?
>
> Why was it wrong?
>
> How did it hurt the other person?
>
> What was your goal?
>
> What's a better way to achieve that goal in the future?

- If the bullying continues, seek professional counseling for your teen right away. As many as 60% of habitual bullies wind up in trouble with the law.

What can parents do if their own kids are being bullied?

- Realize that your teen needs your support. Avoid criticizing him as being weak or unable to stand up for himself. He needs to know that at least his parents think he is a worthwhile person.

- At the same time, avoid the tendency to pity and make excuses for your teen. That will not do any favors for his self-esteem, either.

- If the bullying is not severe, use your Active Communication skills (Chapter 2) to help empower your teen to handle the problem himself.

- With more severe or ongoing bullying, talk with the school counselor, a teacher, or someone in the school administration. Work together and follow through to make sure the bullying stops.

- Get support for your teen through a peer group of others who have been bullied. A school counselor or a private therapist can help you locate a group that meets in your area.

What can bystanders do?

Most bullying takes place when other kids are around. Most of these "bystanders" would like to help but don't know how. Talk with your teen about how to help and when. Emphasize that if the situation is too dangerous, she should get adult help.

- *Walk away.* This lets the bully know that what they are doing is not funny or acceptable.

- *Take a stand.* Tell the bully that what he is doing is wrong. By saying, "That's not cool. Let's get going," or something similar, kids can stand up for each other. This may also give other bystanders the confidence to speak up or walk away.

Reach out. Sometimes kids get picked on because they don't have any friends or anyone to stand up for them. When kids befriend someone being bullied, bullies are less likely to pick on them. Friendship can also give teens the support and the confidence to stand up for themselves.

Spread the word. When more kids stand up to bullies, they are less likely to continue their behavior.

Get help. Some situations are too dangerous to handle alone. Make sure your teen knows it is important to get adult help when the bullying is either violent or ongoing.

10 Prevention Strategies for Parents

Strategy #9. Identify and confront high-risk behavior.

Preventing drug use, reckless sexuality, violence, and other high-risk behaviors is more than a matter of setting guidelines and hoping for the best. As the saying goes,

You get what you <u>inspect</u>, not what you <u>expect</u>.

In other words, it takes some vigilance on the part of parents to make sure there teen is keeping his agreements and behaving safely. Is your teen going to parties where drugs or alcohol are present? Is she smoking cigarettes behind your back? Is he hanging out with friends who shoplift or bash mailboxes for fun? To find out, you have to keep your eyes open—and your mind open, too. In other words, beware of convincing yourself so well that your teen "would never do that," you don't recognize the signs when he does.

Let's explore the process of identifying and confronting high-risk behavior in your teen. We'll focus on one of the biggest problems that parents of teens worry about: the use of tobacco, alcohol and other drugs. First, we'll get an overview of the problem.

Stages of Drug Use

Drug use frequently progresses in four stages:

1. Experimentation

Nearly 90% of all teens will try alcohol or marijuana. This is not to say that all of them suffer from low self-esteem and discouragement. The majority are motivated by simple curiosity. They have seen alcohol used by the adults in their lives and have watched alcohol and drugs used in TV and movies for years (often, unfortunately, in an overly glamorized way). They wonder what it's like. They see that "everyone tries it" and don't want to be the only one who hasn't.

2. Social Use

About three-fourths of the teens who enter the experimentation phase move on to stage two—social use. These teens will use alcohol and other drugs at parties and other social settings, often mimicking behavior they see around them.

3. Seeking

In this third phase, teens will actively seek out places where drugs can be found. It is usually in this phase that addiction begins.

4. Habitual Use

Teens who move into the habitual use phase are now driven primarily by the desire to use the alcohol or other drug, despite negative consequences or harmful effects. It has become an addiction, often both physical and psychological. The addict's free will is overwhelmed, and reason takes a back seat to the need to feed the addiction.

Fortunately, although a teen can go through all four stages in just a few months, the progression is not inevitable. Drug use can be stopped at any stage; however, the more involved young people are with drugs, the more difficult it is for them to stop. The best way to fight drug use, therefore, is to prevent it from starting in the first place. Educating teens about the harmful effects of drugs long before the teen years is ideal. If that isn't possible, however, there is still a lot that you can do.

We talked about the importance of establishing a no-use rule in your family. This is a good starting place, but for any rule to be effective, the parent must be willing to expend the energy to detect when it is being violated.

Four Signs that a Teen is Using Alcohol and Other Drugs

- Heavy identification with the drug culture (drug-related web sites, music, slogans on clothing, conversations and jokes that suggest preoccupation with drugs, hostility when discussing drugs)

- Signs of physical deterioration (memory lapses, short attention span, difficulty in concentration, poor physical coordination, slurred or incoherent speech, unhealthy appearance, indifference to hygiene and grooming, bloodshot eyes, dilated pupils). Again, some of these signs are often the effects of harmless teenage behavior, but when many of them appear together, it's time to suspect alcohol or other drug use.

- Dramatic changes in school performance: a distinct downward turn in your teen's grades (not just from C's to F's, but also from As to Bs to Cs), more and more uncompleted assignments, and increased absenteeism or tardiness

- Changes in behavior such as chronic dishonesty (lying, stealing, and cheating); trouble with the police; changes in friends; evasiveness in talking about new friends; possession of large amounts of money; increasing and inappropriate anger, hostility, irritability, and secretiveness; reduced motivation, energy, self-discipline, and self-esteem; a diminished interest in extracurricular activities and hobbies

Although all of these symptoms have been found to be associated with alcohol and other drug use, you should not draw conclusions on the basis of one or two of them. Look for an overall pattern of behavior.

One of the best ways to determine whether teens are using alcohol or other drugs is to notice their behavior when they come in at night. Do they act incoherent or odd? Do you smell alcohol on their breath? Are their pupils dilated? By being observant, you may be able to determine not only whether your teen is hanging around peers who use alcohol and drugs, but whether he is actually using them himself.

In any discussion of detection, parents always ask whether they should search a teen's room. I believe we should show our teenagers the same respect that the law, in general, shows us. A police officer may not come into your home and go through your belongings without probable cause and a search warrant; similarly, you ought not to make a routine habit of searching your teen's belongings. However, if you have reasonable grounds to believe that your teen is harmfully involved with alcohol or other drugs, I do believe you have the right to go through his belongings in search of hard evidence with which to confront him.

Three signs almost always mean that your teen is becoming involved with drugs:

"Hard Evidence" of Drug or Alcohol Involvement

- Possession of drug-related paraphernalia such as pipes, rolling papers, small decongestant bottles, or small butane lighters

- Possession of drugs themselves or evidence of drugs (peculiar plants, butts, seeds, or leaves in ashtrays or clothing pockets; small plastic bags or vials; pills[1])

- The odor of alcohol or other drugs or the smell of incense or other cover-up scents

---

1. Several reliable web sites exist that can help you identify unknown pills that you may find in your teen's possession. Pharmaceuticals can usually be identified by the numbers or letters that have been imprinted on the pill. Pills such as Ecstasy, which are created in illegal labs, may not be in a pharmaceutical database, but an Internet search for the pill's shape, color, or imprinted marks might still turn up useful information.

Consider that it is almost impossible to find out whether a teenager is involved with alcohol or other drugs by asking. By becoming involved, the teenager has probably already made a decision to lie. He is therefore likely to say "no" whether he is using or not. As a last resort, the availability of drug screening through hospitals, labs, drug treatment centers, and at-home urine-collecting kits can offer you a way to clarify whether or not you teen is using drugs. However, drug-testing is not a substitute for any prevention strategy.

Confronting Your Teen

Parents frequently deny evidence of drug use and postpone confronting their teen. The earlier a drug problem is found and faced, the easier it is to overcome.

If you suspect your teen of using alcohol or other drugs, you must first deal with your own anger, resentment, and guilt. Do not take your teen's alcohol or other drug use as a sign that you are a bad parent. Remember that parenting is not the only influence on a teen's development.

Do not try to have a confrontation while your teen is under the influence of a drug. If your teen is unconscious or semi-conscious, take him immediately to a detoxification center or a hospital emergency room. Since alcohol poisoning can be fatal, do not make the mistake of allowing your teen to "sleep it off." Teens will also mix alcohol with more dangerous drugs, so you do not know what else may be in his system. In addition to the medical importance of seeking treatment, it also sends your teen the clear message that drug use is serious business and that you are not going to take it lightly.

Be careful not to react with rage or excessive anger. Although you may feel justified in becoming angry, a calm, firm reaction produces the best results. Trying to humiliate your teen is also likely to be counterproductive. Bribery does not work, either. The teen will, most likely, take the rewards but continue to use alcohol or other drugs. Threats and unreasonable discipline also tend to drive the teen further into alcohol or other drug use.

When you confront out of caring ("I'm doing this because I care about you") and not from anger, your teen is much more likely to respond positively.

When you need to confront a teen about drug use, what works best is the use of solid communication with logical consequences—the same skills recommended for other violations of guidelines and limits. The key is to be firm, calm, and caring. When you confront out of caring ("I'm doing this because I care about you") and not from anger, your teen is much more likely to respond positively.

Remember to act more and talk less. Lectures almost always fall on deaf ears when a teen is already involved in alcohol or other drugs. But when you follow through with the logical consequences that you and your teen agreed upon, you'll capture your teen's attention.

It is essential that you present a unified front with your spouse, as any disagreement between the two of you can be exploited by your teen.

If you are married or live with a partner, try to come to an agreement about how to handle the situation. It is essential that you present a unified front, as any disagreement between the two of you can be exploited by your teen. Sit down together and plan how you will confront your teen. A single parent may want to ask an adult friend or relative to assist in the confrontation. You may find strength in numbers. Review the evidence you have found and decide how to present the information to your teen in a respectful, yet forceful, manner. It is important that you back up each accusation with examples and evidence.

Think about your goals for the confrontation. If your teen appears to be in the early stages of drug use, your goal might be to obtain an agreement to cease all use. If your teen is already in the addicted or heavy-use stage, your goal will be to get her into a treatment program. Consult your local mental health center, a physician, or a hospital that specializes in alcohol or other drug use. Also ask your teen, since he or she still has a choice in the matter. If you are not sure how far along she is—which is often the case—your goal may be to get her to go for an evaluation, where a professional can help you make the determination. Again, the easy availability of drug screening can help you monitor your teen's future use.

Suicide Threats

Be prepared for your teen to try to divert you from focusing on his drug use. Teens also tend to lie or make excuses or threats when confronted. They may threaten to run away, to behave even more inappropriately, or even to commit suicide. Take any threats seriously, but do not allow yourself to be blackmailed. It is particularly important to treat a suicide threat seriously. Contact a crisis center, suicide hotline, or mental health center immediately. They can help you assess the situation and determine if the suicide threat is serious or just manipulative. Do not try to make this determination yourself.

Gangs: A Threat to Your Teen?

Not long ago, gangs were mainly a phenomenon of big cities and economically repressed neighborhoods. Now, however, gangs can be found in all 50 states, in suburban areas and small towns, and they draw members from all classes and ethnicities, male and female alike.

Teens are most likely to join youth gangs, as opposed to adult gangs. And while youth gangs rarely run big drug operations themselves, they often sell drugs for adult gangs that do. Youth gangs often expect or even require members to engage in violent and criminal activities as a rite of passage, to defend their turf, or to get money any way they can. Teens who get involved with youth gangs are much more likely than others to eventually join adult gangs.

There are some signs of gang involvement that you can look for in your teen:

Youth Gangs: Signs to Look for in Your Teen

- Graffiti on belongings
- Tattoos, scars, or burns
- Fights at school
- Friends wearing same colors or symbols
- Secretive behavior
- Change of friends
- Use of drugs/alcohol
- Anti-authority attitude
- Unexplained expensive items or large sums of money
- Staying out late

Just like the signs of alcohol or drug use, your teen exhibiting one or two of these signs may not be anything to worry about—just normal teen behavior. Look for a pattern of behavior. If you have friends or neighbors whose teens have become involved with a gang, talk to them about the signs that they noticed. And if you do suspect that your teen is involved with a gang, the next step is to try to talk to him or her about it. The "Confronting Your Teen" section on page 214 contains information that will be useful to you in this situation.

Even if your teen is not involved with a gang, consider having a Problem-Prevention Talk about this issue so that your teen will know exactly where you stand on it. In preparation for any confrontation or prevention talk, it's helpful if you take time to understand the topic as thoroughly as possible.

Why do teens join gangs?

We can identify four main reasons why teens join gangs:

- To belong
- Desire for prestige
- Protection from bullies
- Thrill seeking

You might come up with other reasons, but most will fit within these categories. For example, "To escape from dysfunctional home life" would fit under "To belong." And if you think about how this list compares to the goals of teen behavior that we talked about last session, you will uncover some similarities.

Why Teens Join Gangs		Goal
To belong	➡	Belonging
Desire for prestige	➡	Power
Protection from bullies	➡	Protection
Thrill seeking	➡	Challenge

You can see that some very powerful forces are behind a teen's decision to join a gang. When, for one reason or another, teens have low self-esteem and lack the courage to choose a positive, but more difficult, approach to their goals, joining a gang may seem like an attractive option.

Before you confront a teen about gang involvement or have a problem-prevention talk, understand that the greatest danger of gang culture is that it glorifies violence, criminal activity, and casual sex. Teens buy into the rebellious and thrilling part of gang life without considering the real results: a criminal record, imprisonment, debilitating injury, and even death—not only their own death, but also the death of family members and other innocent people.

The threat of your teens becoming involved with a gang is far too dangerous to let natural consequences teach the lesson. How do you get through to teens about the dangers of gang involvement when risk-taking is part of its allure? As we said before, parents have to become knowledgeable and very persuasive. Gain the knowledge by researching gangs—not only the facts about gang violence, but also the music, language, and attitudes of gang culture. Be persuasive by pointing out the differences between fantasy and reality. The chart below might give you some ideas. With knowledge and persistence, you might just get through to your teen.

Talking to your Teen about Gangs

Fantasy	Reality
"Getting shot will make me seem tough."	Getting shot will make you dead; or you could get "lucky" and live as a vegetable who has to be fed by your parents for the rest of your life.
"Being in a gang will protect me from bullies."	Being in a gang will make enemies of lots ´of people who didn't care one way or the other about you before. You'll be much more likely to get hurt or killed than you were before, and you won't feel safe outside your own neighborhood.
"People will respect me if I'm in a gang."	What you get from being in a gang is fear, not respect. People will only treat you well because they have to, not because they really think you deserve it. And your fellow gang members will only respect you as long as you're willing to commit crimes and hurt other people.
"I'll finally feel like I belong to a real family."	Real families don't force people to commit crimes to get respect and love; they accept and love you for who you are. You won't find that kind of love from a gang. Even if your family is having problems, being in a gang will not solve them—it will only make things worse.
"I'll make a lot of money."	Most gang members don't make much money. Those who do usually end up doing time. Plus, if you're in a gang, it's far more likely that you'll drop out of school because of problems with rival gang members. Getting your education is the key to making money—not joining a gang.

Strategy #10. Calmly manage a crisis, should one occur.

Whether the crisis is a drug overdose, a suicide attempt, pregnancy, or the discovery that your teen has committed a crime or been the victim of one, your calm handling of the situation can make all the difference. Keep the following issues in mind as you manage the crisis.

First, stay calm. Do not blow up or give up. A crisis is not the end of the world, just a larger, more pressing problem. Flying into a rage because your teen has violated your values may drive a wedge between the two of you. Instead, recognize that teens make mistakes, and that your teen needs your support now more than ever. You can discuss differences in beliefs after the crisis has been handled.

Many people are not aware of the resources available in every community and for every budget. Professionals are available immediately by phone (hot lines), while others are skilled at helping resolve problems after the immediate danger has passed. Some of these resources are listed in the back of this book. You can find others by calling your pediatrician or a local mental health center, or by searching through your local yellow pages.

Getting Help

If your relationship with your teen has deteriorated to the point that she is "out of control" (ignores your authority and does what she pleases) or if you suspect that she may be harming herself or is otherwise in danger, you will need to get professional help. Start by calling your teen's school counselor, psychologist, or social worker, the local community mental health center, a private therapist specializing in adolescents, or your family physician. If problems persist, residential treatment in a hospital, therapeutic program, or other setting may be called for. Your first-level helper can assist you in finding a resource that fits your needs and budget. You can also refer to the list of resources in the back of this book, or go to **www.ActiveParenting.com/ParentingTeens** for a more extensive list of resources.

Manage your own feelings.

Feeling guilty will only make it harder for you to handle the situation effectively. A more useful feeling is resolve: *resolve to handle the problem effectively and to learn from the experience.*

Be aware that you may feel overwhelming guilt if your teen reaches a crisis. You may have made mistakes in your parenting (we all have), but remember that it is your teen who is ultimately responsible for her choices. Feeling guilty will only make it harder for you to handle the situation effectively.

A more useful feeling is *resolve*: resolve that you will do what you can to handle the problem effectively and to learn from the experience so you can help prevent such problems in the future. It will help to keep in mind that although you are the most important influence in your teen's life, you are not the only influence.

▲ ▲ ▲

This brings us to the end of our Ten Prevention Strategies for Parents. Each of these strategies is a powerful parenting tool, and when you use them together, you'll be doing your best to prevent your teen from getting involved with risky behavior. Here they are again in list format, for easy review:

Ten Prevention Strategies for Parents

1. Be a positive role model and a teacher of values.

2. Educate teens about the risks.

3. Filter out negative influences and in positive ones.

4. Establish clear guidelines for behavior.

5. Monitor and supervise teen behavior.

6. Work with other parents.

7. Provide healthy opportunities for challenge.

8. Consult about how to resist peer pressure.

9. Identify and confront high-risk behavior.

10. Calmly manage a crisis, should one occur.

Family Council Meetings

Encompassing family talks, the FLAC Method, and many other skills, the family council meeting is a forum in which all family members solve problems and make decisions.

The highest level of family participation and Active Parenting skills come together in the family council meeting. Encompassing family talks, the FLAC Method, and many other skills, the family council meeting is a forum in which all family members solve problems and make decisions. A family council meeting is to a family what a business meeting is to an organization. Typically, a family holds this type of meeting once a week for twenty minutes to an hour, following an agenda.

Family council meetings may be the most challenging of all the Active Parenting skills to use because most families have difficulty fitting meetings into their schedules. It may be hard to find a regular time each week to hold a meeting, but making the effort can pay rich dividends. No other forum allows so much valuable communication among family members.

The Basics of Family Council Meetings

- Who should attend family council meetings? Anyone who has a stake in decisions affecting the daily life of the family should be present, including anyone who lives with the family, such as grandparents, uncles, or aunts. If you're a single parent, avoid discussing any problems the teens have with the absent parent. These are not your problems to solve. Address them at some other time, using the Active Communication process.

- What if a family member doesn't want to attend? Hold the meeting anyway, without that person. He may see later that he is missing out on helping to make important family decisions (many of which will probably affect him).

- Agree on a time and a place. Sunday afternoon or right after Sunday dinner is usually a good time, since the family is more likely to be together then. It's an opportunity to review the past week and look forward to the upcoming week. The dinner table is a great place for a meeting, since everyone has a chair.

- The first family council meeting should be a short one. Try addressing only one issue at this meeting, and plan something fun to do right after the meeting. Later meetings can be longer and follow a more extensive agenda, but the first one is more of a practice.

Leadership Roles

Two people need to be leaders at a family council meeting:

1. The **chairperson**, who keeps the discussion on track and sees that everybody's opinion is heard

2. The **secretary**, who takes notes during the meeting and reads them at the start of the next meeting

You can fill these two roles yourself at the first meeting. After that, other family members should take turns so that no one person is in charge every time.

Overall Agenda

Some families think a formal agenda is too businesslike for a family meeting; however, structuring the meeting around an agenda helps make the meeting a little more special than everyday family life, and it keeps the meeting on track. We suggest the following order of business:

1. **Compliments.** Family members start the meeting by complimenting good work and saying "thank you" to anyone who contributed to a positive event in the previous week. Encourage improvement in behavior. Beginning on this positive note sets a cooperative tone for the meeting and encourages ongoing improvement.

2. **Reading the minutes.** Last week's secretary reads aloud the notes from the previous meeting.

3. **Old business/new business.** Discuss any unfinished topics from the last meeting and address what's on the agenda.

4. **Chores and allowances.** You may choose to discuss family money issues now. Some families pass out allowances at this time.

5. **Treat or family activity.** After the meeting ends, stay together for a game, an outing, or a dessert. This time together helps you have fun, enjoy each other's company, and get the week off to a good start.

New Business Agenda

Most families find that the new business section of the family meeting works better when all items are written on a posted agenda before the meeting. A sheet of paper labeled "Agenda" can be posted on the refrigerator or another convenient location. When a problem occurs that a family member would like handled at the next family meeting, she can write it on the agenda.

Agenda

1. Megan comes into my room without knocking (Ty)

2. Raising allowances (Megan)

3. Planning for the holidays (Mom)

Agenda items that don't get covered in the meeting can be rolled over into the next one. Often family members will solve a problem among themselves before the meeting, so that problem can be dropped from the list.

A written agenda offers parents an excellent way to stay out of their teen's fights. When a teen tries to engage you in solving one of his problems for him, you can sympathetically suggest that he put it on the agenda for that week's meeting.

Example:

Ty: *"Megan keeps coming into my room without knocking. Tell her to stop."*

Mother: *"You sound pretty angry about that. Why don't you put it on the agenda for this week's family meeting?"*

When you address problems such as this during a family council meeting, follow the same guidelines as you would when using the FLAC Method::

Family Meeting Guidelines

- Every person has an equal voice.

- Everyone may share what she thinks and feels about each issue.

- Decisions are made by consensus.

- All decisions are in effect until the next meeting.

- Some decisions are reserved for parents to make.

Just knowing that a forum exists to handle complaints helps many family members feel empowered and more cooperative.

When there are no pressing problems on the new business agenda, you may choose to use this time for a family talk.

Even if you are unable to hold weekly family meetings, I encourage you not to give up on the concept. You can call them "as needed," whenever a family member has an important item to put on the agenda or problem to solve. Just knowing that a forum exists to handle complaints helps many family members feel empowered and more cooperative.

Family Enrichment Activity: In Our Family

Families have been the backbone of civilization for thousands of years, and your family is the most important family in the world…to your children and teens. History has proven time after time that alone we could never survive, but by form-

ing small cooperative units we can thrive. Families are a source of belonging, learning, and contributing for individuals and for society. To a large extent, the measure of any civilization rests on the strength of its families.

So whether you are part of a traditional Mom-and-Dad family, a stepfamily, a single-parent family, a same sex family, or any other type of family, it's important for you to look for ways to let your children and teens know that they are part of a family unit. Plan frequent family activities, use phrases like "in our family," and develop your own family traditions and rituals. Give your children the gift of memories by telling and retelling the special stories of your family's history—stories that make your family unique. Remember, too, that through your family your children will learn that they belong to a much larger family: the family of humankind. And since their contributions to that family will help determine the future of all people, your job as a parent may very well be the most important job in the world.

Letting Go

In the beginning of this book, I stated that the purpose of parenting is to protect and prepare teens to survive and thrive in the kind of society in which they will live. Preparing your teen for a life independent of you is an essential part of being an Active parent. In fact, as important as effective parenting is to the future of any society, it is also one of the few jobs in which the goal is to work yourself out of a job.

It's been suggested that the most difficult task for any teenager is to break away from his parents and eventually return to them as a fellow adult. The skills presented in this book can help set the stage for such a passage. But it will take one more thing: your willingness to let go.

I have used the image of a ship at sea to describe the voyage your teen will take as she leaves the safe harbor of her family for ports unknown. I've spoken of the storms and icebergs she will encounter, and how you can help give her the kind of character she will need as ballast to stay stable in spite of these threats to her safety.

Yet, even with the skills you are developing to help prepare her for a safe voyage, it takes courage for you to let go of the rudder and trust that she has what she needs to make the journey.

The concluding poem is my hope that you will have that necessary courage when the time comes to wish your teen "bon voyage."

A Final Gift:

Letting Go
(to a Teen Leaving Home)

Boats in the harbor are safe near shore
Far from the unknown sea,
But just as boats were made for more,
It's the same with you and me.

Those who would anchor their teens with a stone
In hopes of preventing a wreck,
Find that their fears are never undone
And the stone ends up weighting *both* necks.

So I give to you a port called home
Where your ship was built so strong,
And if you need to harbor here,
You know that you belong.

And I give to you the maps you'll need
That you may set the course
For places that I'll never see,
So go without remorse.

Tilting your sails into the wind
With hope, and vision and courage—
I kiss you once, then touch your chin
And wish you bon voyage!

—*Michael H. Popkin*

chapter **6**

Home Activities

1. Re-read any parts of this book that you need practice with.

2. Role-play with your teen about how to say "No" to peer pressure, using the activity on pages 205-207 for practice.

3. Have a family council meeting. Create an agenda beforehand. Use the tips on pages 221-224 to help you run the meeting smoothly.

Active Communication Activity *Answer Key*

Mother: Hey. You seem pretty miserable. And you've never cut school before.

Abby: Well I'm not going so don't even try.

Mother: You sound pretty upset about it.

Abby: You would be too.

Mother: I see. What happened that's got you so upset?

Abby: Nothing.

Mother: Sometimes it helps to talk about it.

Abby: I doubt it…and it's not going to change my mind about going.

Mother: Well, I can't make you go, Abby. And I don't know what you'll decide to do, but I would like to talk to you about it.

Abby: Well, Steve, he's a senior and the editor of the yearbook and I'm on the staff for the freshman class and he called this big meeting and started yelling about people missing deadlines and stuff and the only person he called out by name was me. And when I tried to tell him my excuse, he cut me off and said this wasn't day care and it wasn't his job to babysit freshmen.

Mother: Oh, Abby...that must have really hurt.

Abby: I wanted to crawl under a desk and die.

Mother: Pretty embarrassing!

Abby: Yeah. I've never been so humiliated. The rest of them thought it was just hilarious. There's no way I can go back there!

Mother: I can see why you'd feel that way.

Abby: You can?

Mother: Sure. I can remember...well, maybe I shouldn't tell you this...

Abby: Come on! I told you...

Mother: Okay, well ...now I was already a senior, and I went to the movies with a date and we parked. All we did was kiss a little, but he told everyone I was really easy and implied we'd done a lot more...

Abby: Ugh. What a jerk.

Mother: Believe me, I called him worse when I found out, and I was incredibly embarrassed by the whole thing.

Abby: Well, what do you think I should do? I can't just call him a jerk. Besides, I have missed some deadlines.

Mother:	So, as your editor he has the right to expect you to handle your responsibilities.
Abby:	I guess… but he didn't have to be such a show-off and embarrass me in front of everyone!
Mother:	No, I agree. That was uncalled for. Well, let's look at your options. You can hang out here the rest of your life with your dad and me...
Abby:	Ugh. No offense.
Mother:	None taken. What else could you do?
Abby:	I could just quit the yearbook. Write him a note or something.
Mother:	You could quit. How would you feel if you did?
Abby:	Like a quitter. And besides that, there's no way I'm going to give him the satisfaction of making me quit.
Mother:	Well that's one way of looking at it. Tell me something, is this Steve guy really a bad person or was he maybe just feeling the pressure of deadlines himself?
Abby:	Both. He's yelled at other people before.
Mother:	I see. Well, there's something you should know about the world of work. Some bosses are like that, and you have to decide whether it's worth it to work for them or go someplace else. Of course, when you miss deadlines, you can get fired, too,
Abby:	Yeah, well I guess he isn't that bad. I mean he does compliment me on my work... sometimes.
Mother:	What if you asked to talk to him and told him how you felt about what happened?
Abby:	Well...
Mother:	I know. It would take a lot of courage. But I've seen you stand up for yourself before, and you've done it without being offensive.
Abby:	Well, I'll think about it.
Mother:	Let me know how it goes.

—TIME LAPSE—

Mother:	Hi, sweetie.
Abby:	Hi, mom.
Mother:	How'd it go at school today? Did you talk with Steve? ✓
Abby:	Nah. I didn't have to. He sort of apologized to all of us for yelling the other day, and he said that we were all doing a good job.
Mother:	Well, then. I'm glad it worked out for you. ✓
Abby:	Thanks.

The *Active Parenting of Teens* Video-Based Program

This Parent's Guide is a component of the *Active Parenting of Teens* video and discussion program, a six-session parenting education course offered on a local level to parents and other caretakers of teens.

Attending the course offers a variety of benefits, including:

- video vignettes which model positive parenting practices and those you should avoid.

- discussion of Active Parenting skills and theory with the group leader and other group members.

- discussion of parenting issues in general with other parents, plus their support and guidance.

- participation in exercises that demonstrate concepts and teach skills (these are fun!).

To participate in a course, contact your local school system, religious organization, hospital or mental health center, or other "helping professional" in your community. If you are interested in starting your own Active Parenting course, or if you would like to order additional copies of this book (quantity discounts available) call us at 800-825-0060. We'll be glad to guide you with help and resources as you strengthen parenting skills in your home, community, and school system.

Visit out web site at **www.activeparenting.com**

Resource Guide

Please visit www.ActiveParenting.com/ParentingTeens for a more extensive list of books, articles, web sites, and other resources.

Articles and Reports

American Academy of Child and Adolescent Psychiatry. *Facts for Families: Teen Suicide.* www.aacap.org/cs/root/facts_for_families/teen suicide

Centers for Disease Control (CDC) *Youth Risk Behavior Surveillance Report*, 2005.

Kaiser Family Foundation. *Survey Snapshot: Substance Use and Risky Sexual Behavior: Attitudes and Practices Among Adolescents and Young Adults.* Menlo Park, CA: The Henry J. Kaiser Foundation, 2002.

National Campaign to Prevent Teen Pregnancy. *Analysis of Teen Pregnancy Data,* 2006.

National Institute on Drug Abuse. *"Monitoring the Future" Report*, 2005.

Nova Scotia Department of Justice. *Gang Prevention: A Resource Guide on Youth and Gangs.* www.gov.ns.ca/just/publications/documents/GangPrevention.pdf

Online safety tips for teens and parents: http://help.yahoo.com/l/au/yahoo7/360/guidelines/safetytips.html

Substance Abuse and Mental Health Services Administration (SAMHSA). *2005 National Survey on Drug Use and Health*, 2006.

The William and Flora Hewlett Foundation. *Facts at a Glance: A fact sheet reporting national, state-level, and city-level trends in teen childbearing,* 2008.

Teen Depression: Signs, Symptoms, and How to Help. www.helpguide.org/mental/depression_teen.htm

Books

Alvy, Kerby T. *The Positive Parent: Raising Healthy, Happy, and Successful Children, Birth-Adolescence*. New York, NY: Teachers College Press and Studio City, CA: Center for the Improvement of Child Caring, 2008.

Ansbacher, H. L. and R. Ansbacher. *The Individual Psychology of Alfred Adler*. New York: Harper Torchbooks, 1964.

Bernal, M. E., and G. P. Knight. *Ethnic Identity: Formation and Transmission among Hispanics and Other Minorities*. Albany: State University of New York Press, 1993.

Dinkmeyer, Don and G. McKay. *Systematic Training for Effective Parenting*. Circle Pines, MN: American Guidance Service, 1976.

Driekers, Rudolf, and V. Stolz. Teens: The Challenge. Des Moines: Meredith Press, 1964.

Ellis, A. *Reason and Emotion in Psychotherapy*. New York: Lyle Stuart, 1962.

Fine, M. *The Second Handbook on Parent Education*. San Diego: Academic Press, 1989.

Garbarino, James and Ellen deLara. *And Words Can Hurt Forever: How to Protect Adolescents from Bullying, Harassment, and Emotional Violence*. New York, NY: Free Press. 2003.

Ginott, Haim. *Between Parent and Teen*. New York: MacMillan, 1965.

Ginsburg, Kenneth R. with Martha M Jablow. *A Parent's Guide to Building Resilience in Children and Teens*. American Academy of Pediatrics, 2006.

Gordon, Thomas. *Parent Effectiveness Training*. New York: Peter H. Wyden, 1970.

Hartmann, Thom. *Attention Deficit Disorder: A Different Perception*. Lancaster, PA: Underwood-Miller, 1993.

Kowalski, Robin M, Susan P. Limber, and Patricia W. Agatston. *Cyber Bullying*. Malden, MA: Blackwell Publishing, 2008.

Melton, Barbara and Susan Shankle. *What in the World Are Your Kids Doing Online?*. New York, NY: Random House, 2007.

Nelson, Jill R. and Sarah Kjos. *Helping Teens Handle Tough Experiences: Strategies to Foster Resilience*. Minneapolis, MN: Search Institute Press, 2008.

Peterson, Jean Sunde. *The Essential Guide to Talking with Teens: Ready-to-Use Discussions for School and Youth Groups*. Minneapolis, MN: Free Spirit Press, 2007.

Popkin, Michael H. *Active Parenting of Teens Parent's Guide*. Atlanta, GA: Active Parenting Publishers, 1998.

———. *Active Parenting Now Parent's Guide*. Atlanta, GA: Active Parenting Publishers, 2003.

Popkin, Michael H. *Taming the Spirited Child.* New York: Simon and Schuster: 2007.

Sunderland, Margot. *The Science of Parenting*. New York: DK Publishing, 2006.

Thomsen, Kate. *Parenting Preteens with a Purpose*. Minneapolis, MN: Search Institute Press, 2008.

Walsh, David. *Why Do They Act That Way? A Survival Guide to the Adolescent Brain for You and Your Teen*. New York, NY: Free Press, 2004.

Willard, Nancy E. *Cyber-Safe Kids, Cyber-Savvy Teens*. San Francisco, CA: John Wiley & Sons, 2007

More Resources
From Active Parenting

These books are available through your bookstore or from Active Parenting. Check our web site for parenting classes on these subjects in your community, or suggest hosting a class to your child's school, a local religious institution, or adult education provider. Want to teach your own parenting class? Ask about our complete, video-based program kits!

by Michael H. Popkin, PhD
Helps parents of children ages 5 to 12 learn to raise responsible, cooperative children who are prepared to meet the challenges of the teen years and independent living. Also available in Spanish.

Check our web site for more help parenting your adolescent!

- parenting styles quiz
- parent's bookstore
- find a parenting class (live or online)
- links for parents of teens

www.ActiveParenting.com/ParentingTeens

Cooperative Parenting and Divorce

by Susan Boyan, MEd, LMFT, and Ann Marie Termini, EdS, LPC
Ease the transition to a positive new role as "co-parents" with this book that will show how to manage anger, negotiate agreements, and protect children from parental conflict.

by Michael H. Popkin, PhD & Elizabeth Einstein, MA, LMFT
Helps parents and stepparents raise children in the challenging stepfamily environment. The program also teaches how to use powerful communication and negotiation skills to strengthen marriage and family.

by Michael H. Popkin, PhD, Bettie Youngs, PhD, EdD, and Jane Healy, PhD
Parent involvement is key to children's success in school, but it doesn't mean doing their homework for them. This book shows how to support a child by promoting good study habits and working with teachers toward your common goal: a well-educated child.

For more information go to www.ActiveParenting.com or call 800-825-0060

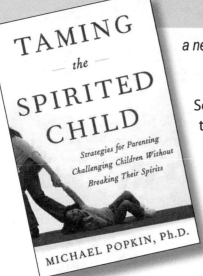

NOTES

NOTES

NOTES

NOTES

NOTES

NOTES

NOTES